INFANT
MASSAGE

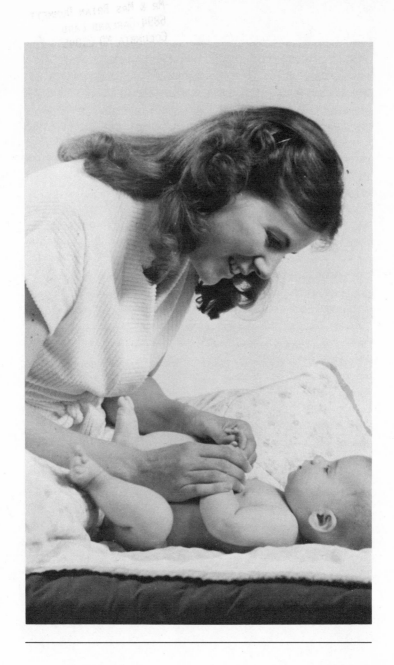

INFANT MASSAGE

A Handbook for Loving Parents

VIMALA SCHNEIDER

Bantam Books
Toronto · New York · London · Sydney

ACKNOWLEDGEMENTS

Thanks to: Celie Tucker Lansing for ideas
on visualizations and healing.
Carol McCarthy, Ron Schneider,
and Ac. Yatiishvarananda Avt.
for support and encouragement.
Special thanks to Thelma Lager.

INFANT MASSAGE: A HANDBOOK FOR LOVING PARENTS
A Bantam Book / September 1982

PRINTING HISTORY
Originally published by Monterey Laboratories, Inc.

Bantam Books are published by Bantam Books, Inc.
Its trademark, consisting of the words "Bantam
Books" and the portrayal of a rooster, is Registered
in U.S. Patent and Trademark Office and in other
countries. Marca Registrada. Bantam Books, Inc.,
666 Fifth Avenue, New York, New York 10103.

PRINTED IN THE UNITED STATES OF AMERICA

0 9 8 7 6 5 4 3 2 1

To
Shrii Shrii Anandamurtiji

and to
all the little children
who shared their Light with me

especially my beloved
Narayana and Sadhana

Frail newborn wings,
Small voice that sings,
New little beating heart,
Dread not thy birth,
Nor fear the earth—
The Infinite thou art.
The sun doth shine
The earth doth spin,
For welcome—enter in
This green and daisied sphere.
Rejoice—and have no fear.

—RICHARD LeGALLIENNE

Contents

Foreword

I nfant Massage is a rare and beautiful gift for young
parents, aiding them in their own gift for their
young children—caring touch.
   Research findings abound showing that the
unfolding of human potential depends on a nurturant
climate during childhood. Touch, beginning at day
one, is a vital component of that climate. And what
better method of intimate human contact than through
daily massage, carefully learned and carefully applied.
Vimala Schneider's book, based on years of study,
practice, and teaching, aids parents in learning the
whys and hows of infant massage.
   Research leaves little doubt on another, less
pleasant matter. External pressures are sure to mount
as we approach the end of this century and prepare for
the twenty-first: economic instability, energy shortages,
threat of war, pollution, crime, galloping change, and
more. Already, experts estimate that stress plays a part
in 60 to 90 percent of all illnesses. The threat of
ever-mounting stress looms large.
   Young adults, then, face twin challenges. First,
their own well-being depends upon maintaining a
personal buffer against stress. A good buffer includes,
for example, regular aerobic exercise, good nutrition,
adequate sleep, a social support network, practice of
deep relaxation, and clear beliefs and values. Effective
stress prevention is identical, then, to effective
preventive medicine.

Second, young parents face the growing challenge of preparing their children to flourish in tomorrow's world of pressure and uncertainty. Perhaps a parent's greatest gift is a climate of love, encouragement, and warmth. Such a climate yields fruits of self-esteem and freedom from an unnecessary buildup of body tension. Caring touch through infant massage can prove invaluable, then, not only in healthy personality development, but in early practice of stress control for the child. And mothers and fathers surely will find peace and nurturance for themselves through infant massage.

Vimala Schneider recently came to my hospital-based Stress and Health Center to train ten West Coast instructors in how to teach new mothers techniques of infant massage. Since then, one of her trainees has begun her own classes with mothers at our center. I was highly impressed with Vimala's depth of understanding about child development, bonding, human anatomy, stress management, and more. I was even more impressed by the enthusiasm and skill she instilled in her trainees and in mothers who participated with their babies in the weekend. The infants obviously enjoyed the experience.

Fortunately, *Infant Massage* now brings Vimala's teachings to a broader audience. New mothers and fathers will benefit. Their babies will benefit even more, now and in years to come. And since our future rests in their hands, Vimala's book is a gift of love for us all.

Walt Schafer, Ph.D.
Director
Stress and Health Center
N. T. Enloe Memorial Hospital
Chico, California

Preface

During the past decade physicians have reassessed the importance of maternal-infant bonding in relation to development. Studies conducted at the University of Colorado and elsewhere have demonstrated that infants whose mothers have difficulty in touching, cuddling or talking to their infants during the first few months of life are more likely to suffer from developmental or growth delay. Scientific advances in the understanding of newborn and infant sensory, motor and cognitive processes have resulted in new appreciation for many of the cultural parenting practices of the nonindustrialized world. For example, the infant carrier packs such as the Snugli are modeled after practices observed in many parts of Africa and Latin America. These infant carriers promote mutual feelings of comfort and security associated with close body contact and still provide the parent with freedom of movement.

In her book, *Infant Massage: A Handbook for Loving Parents,* Vimala Schneider introduces us to a form of parenting which has been practiced for centuries in India. The value of infant massage as a parenting technique can be appreciated best by recognizing the maternal-infant interaction as displayed in the faces of Vimala and her baby shown in the pictures in this book. Hopefully, parents will accept infant massage into the American way of life in the same way that Lamaze childbirth classes and infant carriers have been accepted. An added plus to infant massage is the opportunity it provides to the father, especially of a breastfed baby, for positive interaction with his child.

As a pediatrician, the best advice I can give you is to try the techniques described in this book. If the interaction between you and your child is enjoyable and the massage is fun, you will be providing your infant with a pleasurable form of stimulation which may build a strong foundation for your child's development.

Stephen Berman, M.D.
Chief of General Pediatrics
University of Colorado Health Sciences Center

Introduction

While traveling and studying in India, in 1973, I made a discovery that was to substantially redirect my future family life.

I became aware of the importance of the traditional Indian massage, both for its soothing effects and for its role in affectionate nonverbal communication. An Indian mother regularly massages everyone in her family, and passes these techniques on to her daughters.

Though I noticed how cuddly, relaxed, and friendly the Indian children appeared to be, it remained for me to become pregnant a few years later before I started seriously thinking about the advantages of infant massage.

During my pregnancy, I became interested in all aspects of childbirth and infant development, and began studying everything I could find. Dr. Frederick Leboyer had just written *Loving Hands* (his book on Indian baby massage) and was in town on a lecture tour. After seeing his film on the subject, my fond memories of India vividly returned.

Right then and there, I knew I wanted to massage my baby. After studying all available research on bonding, touch, and infant development, I was surprised that massage wasn't used more widely, because the benefits seemed so obvious.

At that time, I had some friends who were studying Swedish massage. After receiving some delightful massages, I asked them to teach me their techniques.

In 1976, when my baby was three weeks old, I began massaging him. Having taught yoga for five years, I found that a number of these massage techniques were easily incorporated into our daily routine—a routine based on a combination of Indian and Swedish methods. This joyful blend provided my son with a wonderful balance of outgoing and incoming energy, of tension release and stimulation. Additionally, it seemed to relieve the painful gas he had been experiencing that first month.

When I massaged him, he appeared to relax and was happier for the rest of the day. When I stopped massaging him for two weeks, the change was noticeable. From that point on, I decided that massage would remain a permanent part of our lives—not just simply as a tool for relaxation, but as a key part of our communication with one another.

When my son was seven months old, I decided to develop a curriculum and share my discoveries with other parents. Since then more than three hundred mothers and many fathers have participated in my classes. Over the years, they and their babies have provided me with continuing education and inspiration for which I am most grateful.

ON PICKING THE RIGHT WORD

Like many of today's authors, I have encountered the male-female pronoun problem. When referring to a baby, do I say "he or she"? Or "he/she"? Or "s/he"? All of these seem clumsy and forced.

So, to get my own message across as simply as possible, I have chosen to refer to the baby as "he" some of the time, and "she" some of the time—providing balance for all!

Another problem was in reference to the person massaging the baby. I have used Mother as the primary masseuse in the book both for the sake of convenience, and because, in my experience, she is most often principally involved in this care. However, since it is my sincere hope that fathers may be equally interested and involved, I have included a special section for them. To those fathers who read the book and decide to massage their babies, I would simply ask that, in their minds, they change "Mother" to "Father" at the appropriate places.

Enough said!

Vimala Schneider

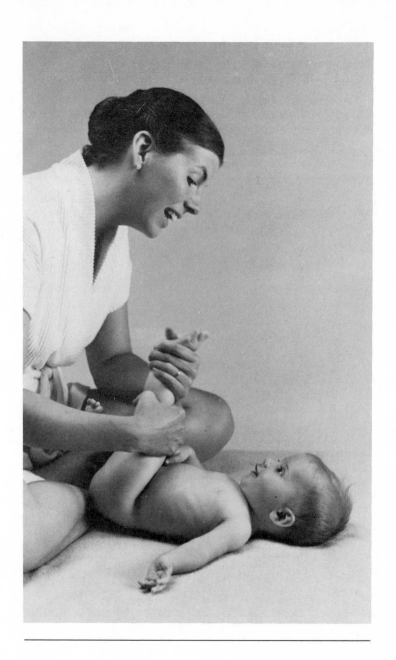

Why Massage
Your Baby?

Being touched and caressed,
being massaged, is food for the infant.
Food as necessary as minerals,
vitamins and proteins.
                    —DR. FREDERICK LEBOYER

A young mother gently cradles her baby in her
lap as the afternoon sun breaks through
cracks in the wooden door. For the second
time that day, she carefully removes the tiny cap and
begins to unwrap the swaddling bands of soft white
linen and wool.

Free from his snug encasement, the baby kicks
and waves his little arms, listening for the now familiar
swish-swish of the warm oil in his mother's hands, and
the comforting sound of her balmy lullaby. So begins
his twice-daily massage.

The scene is in a Jewish *shtetl,* one of the small
enclaves in Poland in the early nineteenth century, but

we could be anywhere in the world, in any century, for it is a familiar tableau of motherhood in every culture throughout the ages.

From the Eskimos of the Canadian Arctic to the Ganda of East Africa; from South India to Northern Ireland, in Russia and Sweden and South America; in South Sea Island huts and modern American homes, babies are lovingly massaged, caressed, and crooned to every day. Mothers all over the world know their babies need to be held, carried, rocked, and fondled. The gentle art of infant massage has been part of the baby caretaking traditions passed from parent to child for generations. Asked why, each culture would provide different answers. Most would simply say, "It is our custom."

Many of the family customs of our ancestors, turned aside in the early twentieth century in the interest of "progress," are returning to our lives as modern science rediscovers their importance and their contribution to our infants' well-being. These include natural childbirth, breastfeeding, rocking (and the cradle), early parent-infant closeness, and massage. Indeed, our great-great-grandmothers would stand up and utter a great "I told you so!" were they to observe our "new" discoveries in infant care.

It is not to our discredit that we need to know why. That question has begun most of the greatest achievements in the history of human knowledge. Knowing why, we will be less quick to cast adrift customs which enrich our lives in a deeper sense than pure sentiment.

Both for babies and parents, the benefits of infant massage are more far-reaching than may at first be obvious. For infants, massage is much more than a luxurious sensual experience. It is a tool for

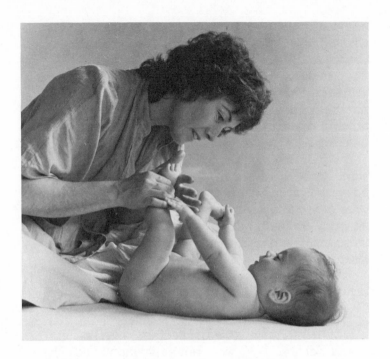

maintaining the child's health and well-being on many levels. For parents, it can be an aid to feeling secure in one's own ability to do something positive for—and get a positive response from—this squealing bit of newborn humanity suddenly and urgently put in our charge.

Physically, massage acts in much the same way in humans as licking does in animals. Skin sensitivity is one of the earliest developed and most fundamental functions of the body. Stimulation of the skin is, in fact, essential for adequate organic and psychological development.

You may wonder why I start out talking about babies and now quickly switch to animals. It is because scientists have seen behavior and responses in animals which parallel the growth and development of our own young. And these parallels are truly fascinating!

In animals, the genitourinary tract will not function without the stimulation of frequent licking. Even the number of times a mother licks her young, and the amount of time spent in each region is genetically determined.

Where the infant animal receives early skin stimulation, there is a highly beneficial influence on the immunological system. In one experiment, rats that were gently handled in infancy had a higher serum antibody standard in every case. More simply stated, these animals had a much greater ability to resist disease.

Equally important for our purposes was the behavior of these gentled rats. In his book, *Touching,* Dr. Ashley Montagu reports:

... When handled, the gentled rats were relaxed and yielding. They were not easily frightened. The laboratory attendant had raised them under conditions in which they were frequently handled, stroked, and had kindly sounds uttered to them, and they responded with fearlessness, friendliness, and a complete lack of neuromuscular tension or irritability. The exact opposite was true of ungentled rats ... these animals were frightened and bewildered, anxious and tense. ...

Among other important findings with the rats: Those who were "gentled" for three weeks after weaning showed a faster weight gain than ungentled rats under the same conditions, and those who were handled gently were physically much more resistant to the harmful effects of stress and deprivation.

When it comes to the licking behavior, Mother Nature has drawn a very firm "bottom line" between life and death for the newborn rats, for, as mentioned before, internal organs in the genitourinary tract will not function in the absence of licking.

Moving up the animal scale, dogs, horses, cows, dolphins, and many other animals have also shown remarkable differences when lovingly handled in infancy. The touch of the human hand improved the function of virtually all of the sustaining systems (respiratory, circulatory, digestive, eliminative, nervous, and endocrine), and changed behavior patterns drastically, reducing fear and excitement thresholds, and increasing "touchability," gentleness, friendliness, and fearlessness.

In *Touching,* Dr. Montagu writes: "... the more we learn about the effects of cutaneous [skin] stimulation, the more pervasively significant for healthy development do we find it to be."

Stimulation of the skin—handling, cuddling, rocking, and massage—increases cardiac output, promotes respiration, and develops the efficiency of the gastrointestinal functions of the human infant (a benefit especially appreciated by the "colicky" baby and his parents).

Nature begins the massage before the baby is born. First, the little one rocks and floats, then slowly his world surrounds him ever more closely. The gentle caress of the womb becomes stronger, turning into contractions which rhythmically squeeze and push, providing massive stimulation to the infant's skin and organ systems.

As opposed to the extremely short labors of most other animals, it has been suggested that a human mother's extended labor makes up for the lack of postpartum licking. For the human infant, the contractions of labor provide some of the same type of preparation for the functioning of his internal systems as early licking of the newborn does for animals.

Touch is also important for the mother. In the previously mentioned studies on rats, if pregnant females were restrained from licking themselves, their mothering activities were substantially diminished.

Additionally, where pregnant female animals were gently handled each day, their offspring showed higher weight gain and reduced excitability, and the mothers themselves showed greater interest in their offspring, with a more abundant and richer milk supply.

Evidence supports the same concepts in humans. Mothers who have meaningful skin contact during pregnancy and labor tend to have easier labors and are more responsive to their infants. Touching and handling her baby assists the new mother in milk production, by aiding in secretion of prolactin, the "mothering hormone." And, by regularly massaging her baby, the mother not only sets up a cycle of healthy responses which improves her mothering abilities day by day, but also enhances her baby's well-being, his disposition, and the relationship between the two of them. The process begun at the embryonic stage thus continues, allowing a natural unfolding of the baby's potential within the safe and loving arms of his mother.

STRESS AND RELAXATION

In our great-grandmother's day, when a baby developed a fever the outcome was uncertain. Each century's children have been plagued with some debilitating disease. Though many contagions have been eliminated through improved environmental conditions and medicine, our century is characterized by a more subtle and insidious malady—stress.

Stress can begin to affect a baby even before he is born. The levels of stress hormones constantly present in a woman's bloodstream directly affect her unborn infant, crossing the placenta to enter his own bloodstream. Studies have shown that prolonged tension and anxiety can hamper a pregnant woman's ability to absorb nourishment. Her baby may be of low birth weight, hyperactive, irritable.

Babies born centuries ago in more primitive cultures had the advantage of extended families, natural environments, and relatively little change. Our children, born into a rapidly advancing technological world, must effectively handle stress if they are to survive and prosper. We certainly cannot eliminate stress, nor would we wish to, for in the proper doses it is an essential component in the growth of intelligence. Let's see how this works.

At times of stress, the pituitary gland produces a hormone, called ACTH (adrenocorticotrophic hormone), which activates the adrenal steroids, organizing the body and brain to deal with an unknown or unpredictable emergency. In experiments on laboratory animals, this hormone has been found to stimulate the production of many new proteins in the liver and brain—proteins which seem to be instrumental in both learning and memory. On being given ACTH, the animals' brains grow millions of new connecting links between the neurons (thinking cells). These links enable the brain to process information.

The stress of meeting unknown situations and

converting them into what is known and predictable is essential for our babies' brain development. But stress is only part of the cycle that enhances learning. Without its equally important opposite, relaxation, stress can lead to overstimulation, exhaustion, and shock. When stress piles upon stress without the relief of an equal portion of relaxation, the body begins to shut out all sensory intake, and the learning process is completely blocked.

How does this apply to infant massage? First, massage is one way we can provide our children with relaxing experiences. Through the use of conditioned-response techniques similar to those developed for childbirth by Lamaze and others, we can teach our babies how to relax their own bodies in the face of stress. The ability to consciously relax is a tremendous advantage in coping with the pressures of growing up in modern society. If acquired early in life, the relaxation response can become as much a part of our children's natural systems as the antibodies which protect them from disease.

However, massage provides more than simple relaxation. Watch a mother massaging her infant. You will see both stress and relaxation in the rhythmic strokes and the baby's reactions. The infant experiences all kinds of new sensations, feelings, odors, sound, and sights. The rumbles of his tummy, the warm sensation of increased circulation, the movement of air on his bare skin; all are mildly stressful to him. The pleasant tone of his mother's voice, her smile, and her touch are relaxing and relieve the discomfort of encountering these new sensations. She reassures him that the world outside the womb is, as Dr. Frederick Leboyer says, "still alive, and warm, and beating, and friendly."

The daily massage provides a perfect balance of stress and relaxation for the infant. It offers him practice in adapting to new sensations within the warm security of his mother's arms. Finally, it provides him with an early stress-prevention program which will be valuable to him in years to come.

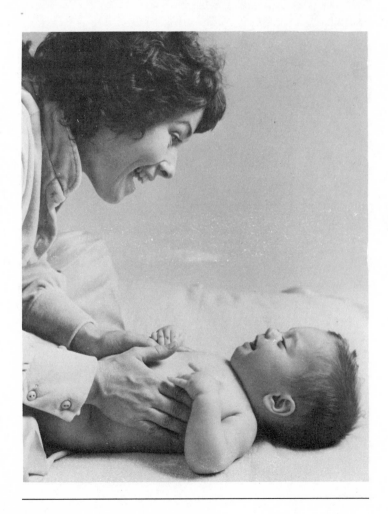

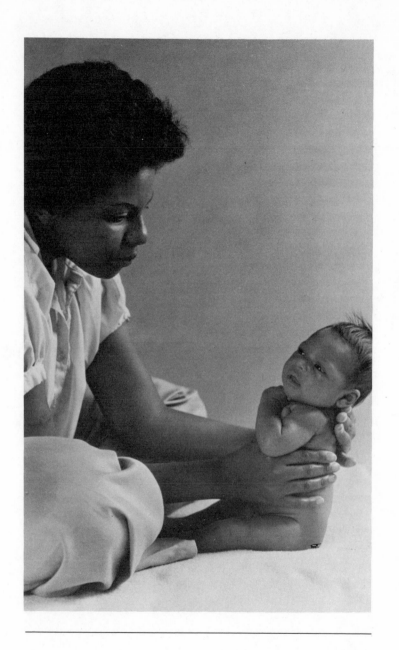

Bonding and Infant Massage

Baby, I lie and gaze on thee
All other things forgot—
In dreams the things of earth pass by,
But awake I heed them not.
I hear thy soft breath come and go,
Thy breath so lately given,
And watch the blue unconscious eyes
Whose light is pure from heaven.

—ANONYMOUS, 1860

An infant's senses develop in sequence; first the proximity senses, those which need the nearness of some object to operate effectively, then the distance senses, those which help her perceive things which are farther away. Of the proximity senses, the first and most important is touch. The sense of touch has been detected in human embryos less than eight weeks old. Though the baby as yet has no eyes or ears, his skin sensitivity is already

11

highly developed. Other proximity senses are taste and smell, both connected with touch and significant to the newborn. A baby only five days old can differentiate her mother's smell and the taste of her milk from that of another mother.

The distance senses, sight and hearing, can be very important to the baby's emotional attachment to his mother, an attachment which is essential to the development of a healthy parent-baby relationship. However, the blind and/or deaf baby will not suffer from lack of this bond; the sense of touch and its impact upon maternal attachment is equally powerful. In fact, it may be more dynamic, because it is the most

significant and highly developed sense.

A mother's instinctive use of a high-pitched voice fits in beautifully with her baby's natural attraction to higher frequency speech. In addition, the beginnings of language learning can be seen in a baby's movement of her body in rhythm and synchrony with her mother's speech patterns, intonations, and pauses. So hearing, as well, plays a part in this early "mating dance" of mother-baby interaction.

Let's take a look at bonding and the attachment process, and see how it is enhanced by the baby's daily massage.

In animals, the crucial period for bonding is usually a matter of minutes or hours after birth. The mother bonds with her infant through licking and touching, which, in turn, helps the infant to physically adjust to extrauterine life. If mother and infant are separated during this time and then are subsequently reunited, the mother will often reject or neglect her young. As a result, the newborn may die for lack of mother's stimulation, even if fed by other means.

In studies paralleling animal behavior, researchers John Kennell and Marshall Klaus, among others, have revealed that there is also a sensitive period for bonding in humans; however, the crucial period seems less rigidly defined and may continue for months, even years after childbirth. *This is truly the beauty of the human species—for we have a marvelous ability to overcome natural setbacks!*

Given the proper tools and encouragement, a mother and her baby can certainly compensate if their bonding has been postponed by separation. But such a mother needs specific awareness of bonding's importance, and the ways to achieve it so that she can *consciously* assist nature. As more and more parents

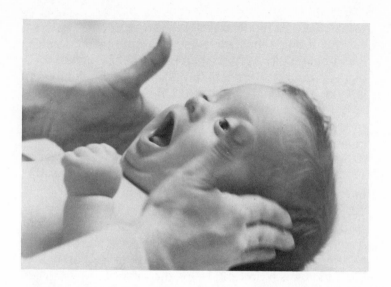

understand the importance of this bond, they will begin taking an active role in enhancing their own attachment to their children.

Unlike the clinging monkey, the human infant has no physical means of initiating contact with her mother and thus getting her needs fulfilled. Her life depends upon the strength of her mother's emotional attachment to her.

Dramatic evidence in the Kennell and Klaus studies correlates the lack of early bonding with later child abuse, neglect, and the failure-to-thrive syndrome (a general physiological and psychological deterioration of an infant with no apparent physiological cause). Mothers who are separated from their infants during the newborn period are often more hesitant and clumsy in learning basic mothering tasks. Even very short separations sometimes adversely affect the relationship between mothers and infants.

Where there is early and extended mother-baby contact, the studies show impressively positive results. Mothers who bonded with their babies in the first hours and days of life later showed greater closeness to their infants, exhibited much more soothing behavior, maintained more eye-to-eye contact, and touched their babies more often. Early-contact mothers were more successful in breastfeeding, spent more time in looking at their infants during feeding, and their babies' weight gain was greater. These children had significantly higher IQ scores on the Stanford-Binet Test at age 3½ than children who had been separated from their mothers.

Clinical data is beginning to show us what many mothers all over the world have known for generations—that loving, touching, nurturing contact between mother and infant has a very real impact upon the child's subsequent development. In short, the attachment of a mother to her newborn is not merely sweet sentimentality—it is a demonstrated biological necessity.

The important elements that help form the bond between mother and infant include eye-to-eye contact, skin-to-skin contact, the mother's voice and baby's response to it, odor, rhythms of communication and caregiving, the activation of maternal hormones by contact with the baby, temperature regulation, and the immunizing bacteria and antibodies transferred to baby by close contact with her mother.

Infant massage helps enhance this bond. Baby learns to enjoy the wonderful comfort and security of loving and being loved. She acquires knowledge about her own body, as mother shows her how to relax a tense arm or back, or helps her to release some painful gas. Mother looks into her eyes, sings, and talks soothingly as she gently strokes her baby's skin. Thus

15

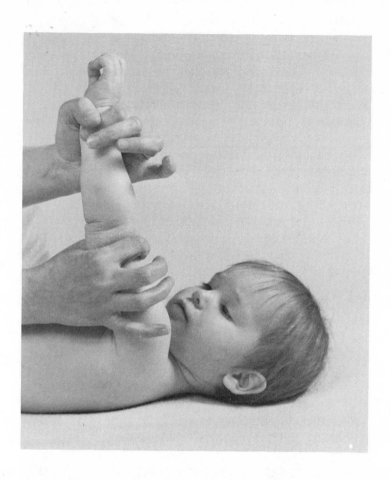

the dance of bonding begins all over again.

The daily massage provides a time for a parent to become intimately acquainted with the baby's body language, her rhythms of communication, her thresholds for stimulation, and how her body looks and feels when she is tense or at ease.

Bonding research also points out that parents feel closer to their infants if they can evoke a positive response from a specific series of actions. Massage, which combines intimacy, communication, play, and caretaking, can greatly enhance a parent's feeling of competence. Setting aside a time for touching and caressing, a mother sends her baby a very special message that says, "I love you and want to communicate with you, and you alone." From all my work, I can say that most babies do indeed get the message!

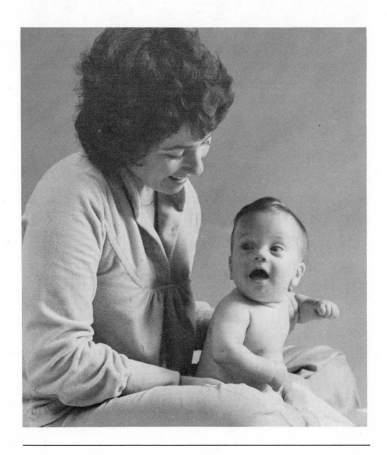

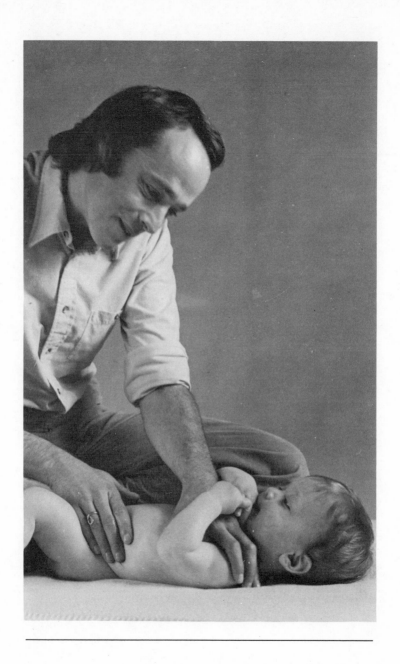

Especially for Fathers

Our little bud of Paradise
Is wakeful, father. I suppose
His clever brain already knows
That if he bubbles long enough
His head will lean against the rough
Attraction of your overcoat.
—NORMAN GALE

Fathers are taking ever-increasing interest in the active care and nurturing of their infants. The image of the clumsy, frightened father who hands baby over to mother until a later, more playful age is fast becoming the exception rather than the rule.

In spite of this eagerness to participate in baby's care right from the beginning, a new father may have logistics problems. Father's time is usually limited to evenings and weekends. He is often tired after work and now must face the added stress of coping with basic household maintenance and increased financial problems.

In the first weeks after birth, his wife may be tired at the end of the day and the baby may be fussy. Father is hard-pressed to find time for himself, and may seem withdrawn at times when mother and baby want and need just the opposite response. Of course, his wife is coping with the same problems, compounded by the sometimes overwhelming responsibility of caring for the baby round-the-clock.

This lack of time, along with a deficit in learned "maternal" behavior, gives Dad two large, but hardly insurmountable barriers in learning to nurture his child with soft and gentle care. Since he has not grown to manhood learning the same behaviors toward babies that most women do, he may need special help and encouragement in the beginning.

Massage is an excellent tool for the father who wishes to round out his relationship with his infant. It is a quality experience for both, from which parent and child benefit immeasurably. Baby learns that Daddy can touch him gently and lovingly; that Daddy, too, is someone he can count on to help satisfy his physical and emotional needs. A father who realizes these qualities in himself, as a result of the massage experience, is certain to have his confidence as a parent substantially boosted.

The most important process that evolves from regular massage is the bonding between a father and his newborn. Just as breast-feeding provides consistent reinforcement of the bonding process for mothers, with its cuddling, skin-to-skin and face-to-face communication, so massaging baby can be just the thing to literally keep father "in touch" with his little one.

Dear Father:

It may be that you will have to structure your time to allow for the twenty to thirty minutes you will need to massage your baby. The best time is usually the morning of your day off, when you can relax unhurriedly. After learning the basic techniques from your wife, this book, or a class, you should be alone with your baby for the massage.

In the beginning proceed very gently, massaging only the chest and stomach or legs. Talk or sing softly, make eye contact as much as possible, and, in general, follow baby's rhythms of communication. As time goes on and your baby becomes more familiar with your touch, you may want to spend more time and move on to other parts of the body, developing your own special massage techniques. For more ideas and helpful hints, please read on, for this book is meant for you, as well.

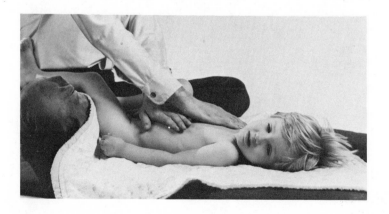

Helping Baby
Learn to Relax

There was a child went forth every day,
And the first object he look'd upon,
    that object he became.
                              —WALT WHITMAN

Close your eyes for a moment, and picture your baby. What do you see? Is he awake or sleeping? Crying? Active or placid? Is he tense or relaxed? Chubby or thin? How does your mental image of him compare with the way he really is right now?

Often we unconsciously form images of ourselves and others, including our children, which are based upon limited experience and evaluation. For instance, my second baby was ill and hospitalized for a little while just after she was born. She came home with a clean bill of health, but for a long time I subconsciously pictured her fragile and weak. Even

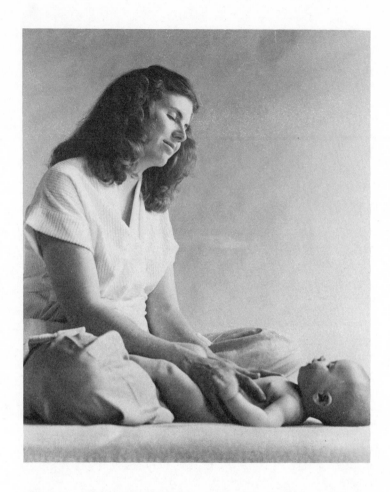

when I realized that I still carried my early fears and projected them onto her, it was difficult to change that image. It had become a habit. These habits of thinking can directly affect those we think about, especially our children, who depend on us for a clear reflection of themselves.

As our thinking is translated into words and

actions, the baby adopts these concepts as his own. Positive visualizations and affirmations can help free us from limiting concepts and give our infants the feedback they need to develop to their full potential. The daily massage is a perfect opportunity to practice positive images and verbal feedback. As you massage your baby, picture him relaxing, opening, letting go of tension. Visualize him happy and healthy. Try to picture his internal organs as you massage; see his heart beating, his lungs healthy, his intestinal tract functioning, gas bubbles moving down and out. Imagine the blood as it moves through his veins and arteries. See your massage facilitating the blood flow to the extremities. Praise his relaxation, his beautiful smile, the softness of his skin. Here are a few examples of statements that help babies adopt positive attitudes about themselves:

"How nice and soft your tummy is!"
"I can feel the gas bubbles moving. Can you help push them out?"
"You are learning how to relax your legs. That's very good!"
"Ah, so relaxed, so loose. You feel so happy now."
"You sleep so deeply after your massage."
"Sarah helps Mommy massage. Such a big girl!"

RELAXATION TECHNIQUES

One of the best things a mother can do for her child is to teach him to help himself. The ability to completely relax is a skill we all could use, and the earlier your child learns it, the more naturally it will come when he needs it. One of the most profound benefits of daily massage that I have seen in my children is the relaxed way they carry themselves. They have been ideal "demonstration models" in my classes because of the way they can relax, even as active preschoolers.

There are a few things you can do during massage time that will encourage your baby to relax. If you attended childbirth preparation classes, you may remember how you consciously rehearsed relaxing each part of your body. You'll be using a similar principle with your baby, calling his attention to an area, showing him how to relax it, then giving him positive feedback as he learns.

For example, let's say you are beginning to massage his arm, and it appears stiff and tense. Take the arm gently at the wrist and give it a little shake, saying to baby in a soft voice, "Relax your arm." Holding the wrist with one hand, use the other to very gently pat the arm up and down, while very lightly shaking it with the other. As soon as you feel any looseness in the arm, give him some feedback, saying, "Good! Very good! You relaxed your arm." Then give him a smile and a kiss. The same thing can be done with other parts of the body. Use very gentle shaking, patting, rolling motions to loosen up the tense area, giving positive "strokes" when you get a favorable response. Not only will this help baby focus his attention on his own body so that later he knows how to relax himself, it will also help him to associate your touch with the positive benefits of relaxation.

ARE YOU RELAXED?

The first few months of your baby's life are happy and exciting, but they can also be stressful. Right now, take an inventory of your body. Which areas are tense?

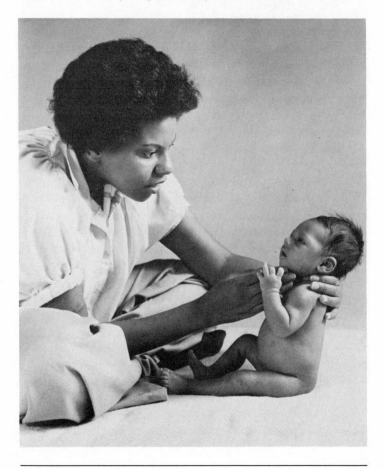

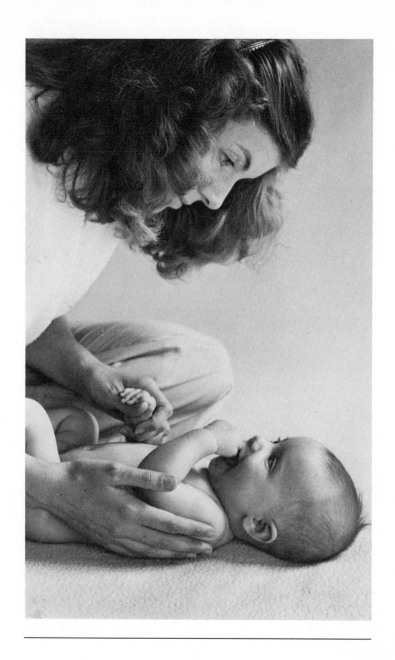

Are you breathing deeply and fully? Perhaps you are holding your baby, nursing, or walking about as you read. Is your baby fussy? When she cries, what happens to your body? Do you tense up, hold your breath? If your baby is sleeping, are you anxious or restive, partially alert for her cries?

The miraculous changes you have undergone during pregnancy and delivery, the demands of caring for a new baby, the lack of sleep and quiet time, all add up to tension and anxiety which can become habitual in the early weeks and months of parenthood. Your baby's daily massage offers a time to relax and unwind. In fact, a relaxed state of mind is essential.

At one time or another, every mother has felt tense and nervous, and in spite of her best efforts baby begins to fuss and cry. Babies are wonderfully sensitive little beings who pick up every nuance of your communication. If you say "relax" with a furrowed brow, baby will get both messages, but the furrowed brow is much more meaningful to her than your words.

Perhaps your baby has a fussy period during the day or evening. Massage her an hour or so before it usually begins to provide her with an outlet for built-up tensions. You will find a simple fifteen-minute massage a welcome respite and transition for the fussy baby/tense mother cycle.

In my son's early infancy, I discovered that massaging him, followed by our taking a warm bath together, helped both of us avoid late afternoon irritability. In the summertime, a massage in the warm morning sun and a splash in the wading pool gave me time for quiet meditation and afforded my baby a wonderful sensory experience.

Music
and Massage

Upon what Instrument are we two spanned?
And what player has us in his hand?
O sweet song.

—RAINER MARIA RILKE

Your voice can be an important part of your baby's massage. By talking softly, humming, or singing, you create an atmosphere of calm; this verbal communication will also help you keep your mind in the present and your attention on the baby.

Singing is a wonderful way to relax. Sing to your baby anytime—changing diapers, feeding, rocking, or walking. You will discover there are some songs your baby loves to hear again and again. His sense of musical discrimination will astound you!

Familiar lullabies from your own childhood would fit in beautifully here. Think of your grandmother's music box that played Brahms' "Lullaby," or the wonderful, lilting "Alouette" you learned in elementary school. Recall how your own mother sang "Go to sleep my baby" to your younger brothers or sisters, and do likewise with your infant.

Here are some folk lullabies from around the world. Undoubtedly you have some family favorites to add to this collection.

Hushabye

American

Hush - a - bye don't you cry, Go to sleep-y lit - tle

ba - by. When you wake you shall take

all the pret - ty lit - tle po - nies. Blacks and bays,

dapples and grays, all the pret - ty lit - tle po - nies.

This is a Bengali chant from India which means, "I love you, my dear baby." Its wonderfully soothing effect on babies has made it a favorite in our infant massage classes. The words are pronounced: Ah-mee toe-mah-kay, bah-lo bah-shee baby.

A - mi to - ma - ke ba - lo ba - shi ba - by. (repeat)

A - mi to - ma - ke ba - lo ba - shi ba - by. (repeat)

Schlaf, Kindlein, Schlaf — German

Schlaf kind - lein --- schlaf, Der va - ter, hüt --- die ---
Sleep ba - by --- sleep. Your fa - ther tends his ---

schaf. Die Mut - ter schuttelts Bau - me - lein, da
sheep. Your mother shakes the dream-land tree, down

fallt her ab ein trau - me - lein. Schlaf kind - lein schlaf.
falls a lit - tle dream for thee. Sleep, ba - by sleep.

Bayushka Bayu — Russian

1. Go to sleep my dar-ling ba - by, ba - yush - ka ba - yu.
2. I will tell you man - y stor-ies, if you close your eyes.

See the moon is shining on you, ba - yushka ba - yu.
Go to sleep my darling ba - by, ba - yushka ba - yu.

Lullaby
Japanese

Shi ba no o - ri-do- no shizu-ga- ya ni
In a hum - ble lit-tle cot-tage with a brush wood gate

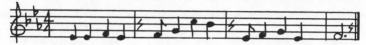

O-ki - na to O---u---na ga su - mai ke --- ri
An old man and his good wife lived in a simple state.

2. Okina wa yama ni   On the mountain every morning
   Shibakari ni   He went gathering wood
   Ouna wa kawa ni   While his old wife washed kimonos
   Kinu susugi.   In the river's flood.

Arrullo Mi Niño
Spanish

Ar - ru - lo mi ni - ño, ar - ru --- lo mi sol.
Lullaby my ba - by, lullaby my sun.

Ar - ru - lo pe - da - zo de mi cor - a - zón.
Lullaby lit - tle piece of your moth - er's heart.

2. Este niño lindo   This pretty little child
   no quiere dormir,   just won't go to sleep,
   el pícaro sueño   that old rascal sleep
   no quiere a venir   just won't come along.

Dors, Mon Petit Enfant
French

Dors mon pe ---- tit en ---- fant, dors
Sleep, lit - tle ba - by mine, sleep

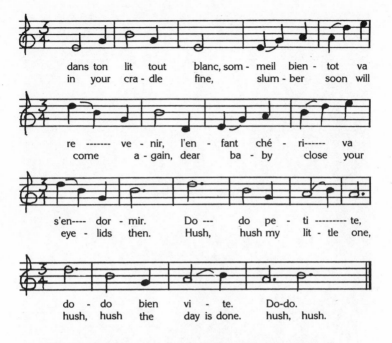

dans ton   lit   tout   blanc, som - meil   bien - tot   va
in   your   cra - dle   fine,   slum - ber   soon   will

re ------- ve - nir,   l'en - fant   ché - ri------ va
come   a - gain,   dear   ba - by   close   your

s'en---- dor - mir.   Do ---   do   pe - ti --------- te,
eye - lids   then.   Hush,   hush my   lit - tle   one,

do - do   bien   vi - te.   Do-do.
hush,   hush   the   day is done.   hush, hush.

If you are not comfortable singing, simply tell a
little story, or talk about the massage as you go. It is
the tone of your voice that is most important, not the
quality of the words and music you project!

Fathers often find the massage time a pleasant
opportunity to play tapes or records or fine radio
music for background music. Guitar music, pleasant
rhythmic tunes which inspire smooth movements,
seem to work best.

Perhaps you have some music in your household
that would offer an accompaniment to your baby's
massage. A soft symphony, the cosmic sound of Paul
Horn's flute, a slow raga of Indian sitar, or the sound of
ocean waves would all provide a beautiful background
for your loving touch.

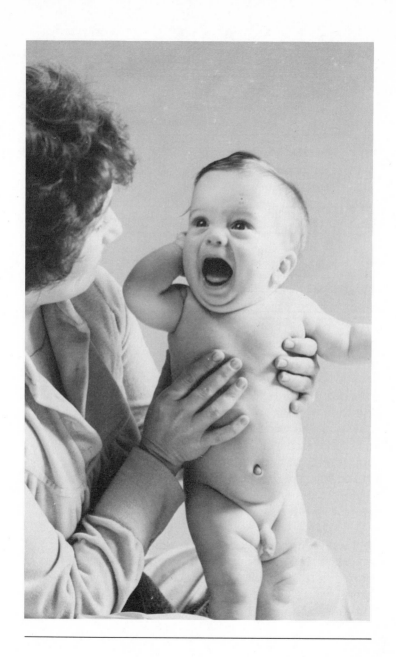

Getting Ready

O young thing, your mother's lovely armful!
How sweet the fragrance of your body!
—EURIPIDES

E ven without conscious awareness, a mother will usually begin massaging her baby, ever so gently, from the moment of birth. It is part of the bonding process—a biological urge to know her baby through all of her senses.

Massages in this book can be started as soon as parents desire. The baby will benefit most by a daily massage for the first six or seven months. As the child becomes more active through crawling or walking, this may be reduced to once or twice a week, as desired. A toddler may enjoy a rubdown before bedtime every night, or after bath time. In this case, it should certainly be continued.

WHEN AND WHERE?

You will want to experiment to find out the time and place that are best for you and your baby. Generally, the morning is a good time to begin, when both of you have been fed and are ready for the day. However, there are also advantages to afternoon and evening massages. For some babies, a massage before a nap is good for releasing that last bit of energy so they can sleep more soundly. For some, however, there is a point of no return—when any stimulation is too much and all the child needs is rest. In this case, give the massage right after the nap. The evening is also a good time for some; if baby is tired but not too cranky, it might also help him to sleep. Your schedule must also be considered. You may work outside the home or have other small children to care for. The evening may be the best time for you, when the day's work is done and your husband can watch the other children for a few minutes. A massage will give you and your new baby the time together that you both deserve.

In the early months, a delightful routine is to massage the baby, then fill a warm bath, and take him in with you. The bath then becomes a wonderfully relaxing experience, and baby may even fall asleep in your arms. To the infant, the experience is rather like a "womb with a view" in that he floats in the womblike warm water, yet, at the same time, sees you as you support him with comfort and security. Baby may cry when you take him out of the tub, but usually some cuddling and/or nursing will quiet him. You may even wish to combine the massage and the bath, massaging him in the tub, using a mild soap instead of oil.

You're probably wondering how both of you get out of the tub safely, and without chills. My method is to keep an infant seat covered with towels next to the tub, and when you are ready to get out, put the baby in the seat, wrapping him with the towels. Then you can both crawl into bed for a nap, or get going with your day.

From six months of age onward, when bath time becomes more of a playtime for baby, the massage works better after the bath, when he is a little more tired, and almost ready for a nap.

Always massage in a warm, quiet place. In the summer, try experiencing the warm morning sun, and the sounds of birds and the smell and feel of the summer air. Take baby to the beach, and massage him with the sound of the water nearby. But take your time . . . your baby is only a baby once.

WARMTH

Peter Wolff, a well-known pediatrician and researcher who completed many studies of newborns and their behavior, observed that temperature has an important effect on the amount of time babies sleep, on their activity, and crying. He found that babies kept at warmer temperatures cried less and slept more than those subjected to cooler environments.

Rudolf Steiner, philosopher, scientist, educator, and propounder of Waldorf Education, also stressed the importance of keeping babies warm. He asserted that the formative forces, both physical and spiritual, which work to help the babies' bodies and souls grow properly, need this warmth to be effective.

I have observed that babies in our infant massage classes, especially those under three months of age, are much more comfortable, startle less, and relax more easily if they are kept quite warm.

If your room is cool, you may want to place a small portable heater nearby. Or you can wrap a baby-size hot water bottle in a towel and tuck it under the blanket near the baby's feet. The room should be warm enough so that you can wear light clothing and still feel warm. Remember, baby has much less bulk to warm him, and without clothing he could be chilled easily.

WHAT YOU NEED

Most mothers are comfortable either sitting cross-legged with baby on a towel in front of them, sitting on the floor or ground with legs extended and baby propped on a towel-covered pillow on mother's legs. The latter position may be more comfortable for a tiny baby, because it will bring him closer to mother's face, and the pillow will make him feel more secure. However, mother should be sure that she can lean against a wall or other back support if she is not accustomed to sitting in this position.

If you have other children around and don't wish to be interrupted, try massaging your baby on the changing table. In this case, you will be standing, so pay special attention to remaining relaxed and

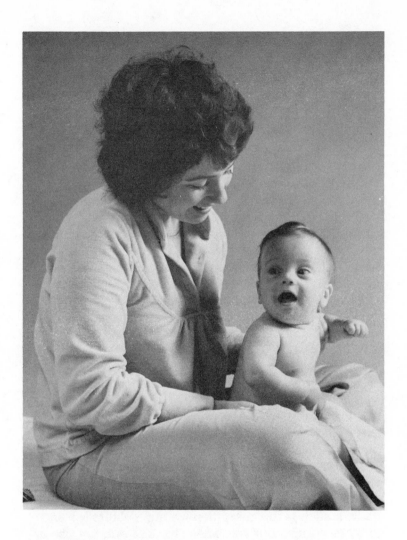

unhurried. If you are massaging in the evening,
candlelight is especially nice.

What else do you need? Massage oil (which we'll
talk about next), towels, a few extra diapers, and a
change of clothes for baby.

WHICH OILS, AND WHY?

As your hands glide over baby's delicate skin, the last thing you want to do is to create any sort of friction.

Most of the time, you will need a light natural oil to work with. The only exception to this might be where baby's skin is very dry, and an oil-based lotion which absorbs into the skin may help soften more easily. But for regular massages, oil is better than lotion because lotions tend to soak into the skin quite rapidly, which means you would constantly have to stop the massage in order to reapply it.

The primary benefit of oil is that it makes the movement smoother on baby's skin. As you are working, you apply the oil generously to your hands. What kind of oil will do the most good for baby, and enhance the stimulating, yet relaxing effects of the massage itself?

For a number of reasons, I prefer cold-pressed fruit and/or vegetable oils, and stay completely away from the mass-produced heavily advertised "baby oils."

From my research in this area, I have developed the belief that a significant amount of what we put on our skin may actually be absorbed deep within the body. If such is the case, then we quite naturally want to try to nourish our little ones topically, and not use a product that may actually rob them of vital nutrients.

Mass-produced "baby oils" have a nonorganic, nonfood petroleum base. Their primary ingredient is mineral oil. To get mineral oil, gasoline and kerosene are removed from the crude petroleum by heating, in a method called functional distillation. By using sulfuric acid, applying absorbents, and washing with solvents and alkalis, hydrocarbons, and other chemicals are then removed.

Not only is there no food value in this type of oil, but it is my personal belief that such a product may actually deplete the system of a number of vitamins, including A, D, E, and K. Some authorities believe that mineral oil, when ingested, produces deficiencies of the vitamins listed above, and specifically recommend against its use as a baby oil. Certainly, when you're in the middle of the massage and baby touches himself, and then puts his hand in or near his mouth, you don't want to worry that such a nonfood substance is passing into his delicate digestive system.

In India, I saw mothers varying the oils they used on their children by the season. In winter, they used hardy mustard oil for warmth. During the summer, they switched to coconut oil for cooling. Apricot kernel and almond oils are two more of my own personal favorites. Not only do such oils keep their vitamins and minerals intact, but also the fatty acids which contribute to healthier skin. Since these oils are nondrying, they will coat the skin rather than be absorbed into it immediately, and this fact makes them excellent for the massage itself.

Such oils are best when used as close to their natural state as possible. For this reason, you might look for the words "cold pressed" on the label. This means that the oil has been extracted only through the use of pressure, without using heat or solvents which drastically change and remove the natural nutrients of the oil.

If the oil you select is enhanced with vitamin E, so much the better, since this vitamin has been shown to be especially healing to the skin. It is also a natural antioxidant, which means that it inhibits the product from rancidity. Cold-pressed oils keep the vitamin E intact; refining through heating or other procedures tends to destroy it.

I stay away from those that have an alcohol base, because they are drying and may cause skin reactions, and remain with the light florals.

There may be times when you've just bathed baby and then choose to massage him. Rather than giving him another bath if his skin is oily after the massage, simply blot him with a soft cloth or towel.

However, very tiny babies can be especially sensitive to any kind of substance put on their skins. Thus my rationale for a natural oil product. Regular bathing will keep baby's pores from clogging and rashes from developing. When in doubt, cleanliness for baby is always best.

THE MASSAGE TECHNIQUE

The massage given here is not manipulative in the way an adult massage by a professional masseur may be; no vigorous kneading here. This massage is a gentle, warm communication. A baby's muscles, comprising only a quarter of his total weight (as compared to almost half in adulthood), aren't developed enough to have knots of tension. His body is so tiny that a short, gentle effleurage is enough to stimulate circulation and tone the internal functions.

In the beginning, while you are learning and your baby is tiny, be very soft and gentle. As baby grows stronger, so should your touch. Do not be afraid to touch your baby firmly; you will find she enjoys being handled and massaged in a manner that communicates your strength, love, and confidence. All of your strokes should be long, slow, and rhythmic, with just enough pressure to be comfortable but stimulating.

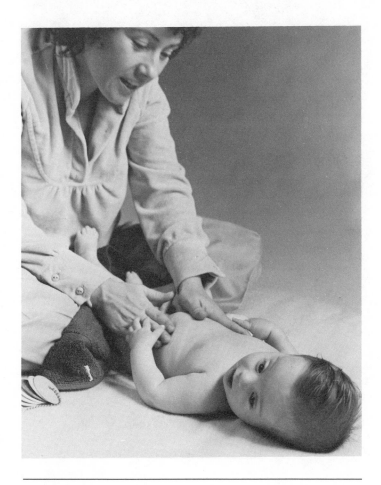

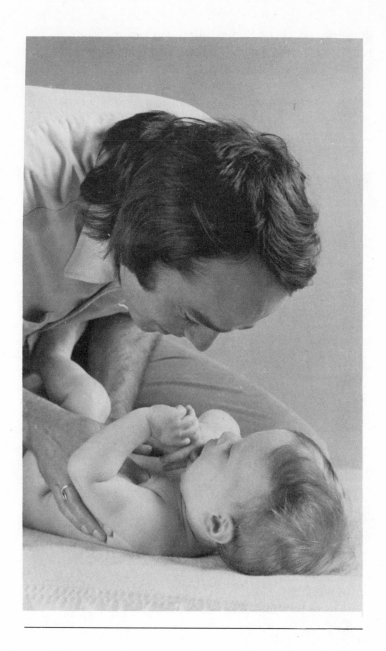

Let's Begin

When from the wearying war of life
I seek release,
I look into my baby's face
And there find peace.

—MARTHA F. CROW

Once you have assembled your tools, find a comfortable spot for the two of you. Then take a few minutes to sit quietly, with your eyes closed or looking at baby. Starting at the top of your head, relax every muscle in your body as much as possible. Feel the wave of relaxation wash over you, from your head to the tips of your toes.

Now gently let your head fall forward so that your chin touches your chest. Slowly rotate your head, first clockwise, then counterclockwise, stretching your neck so that your head sweeps in complete, wide slow circles. Feel all the muscles in your neck and shoulders stretch and relax.

A harmonious mind parallels slow, deep, and regular breathing. As you massage your baby, breathe

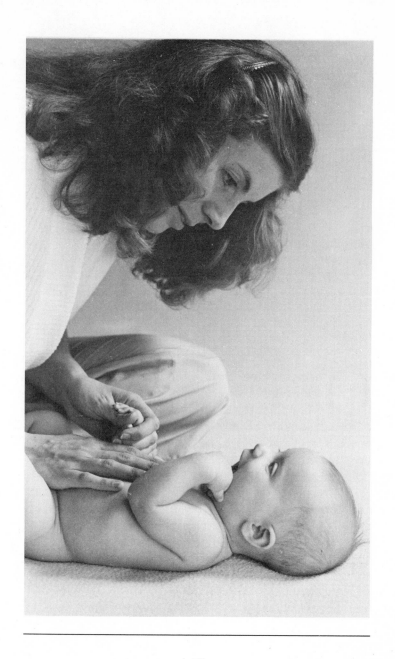

deeply and slowly so that your lungs fill with air and exhalation is complete. Once in awhile, take an audible sigh, breathing in through your nose and exhaling through your mouth, at the same time you consciously relax your body. Your baby will feel this and eventually begin to imitate your relaxing sighs.

Before you begin, take a few deep breaths. With the first breath, affirm, "I now let go of all tension. My body is relaxed." Feel all traces of tension or anxiety leave your body. You are confident and centered.

With the next breath, affirm, "I now let go of all thoughts. My mind is open and free." Let all worries and plans leave your mind, like birds flying through a clear blue sky. You are here, now—just you and your baby. You deserve this time together.

Breathe deeply again, and feel, "I am the gentle power of love, flowing through my hands to (baby's name)." Visualize all the love you have for your baby as a brilliant sun in the center of your heart. With each heartbeat, its warm radiance courses through your arms, into your hands, and over your baby as you begin the massage.

As you massage your baby, every movement of your body will be an expression of your love. Your strong, gentle touch, the rhythm you create, the way you move back and forth with each stroke, your eyes, your smile, your voice, are all as much a part of the experience as the massage itself. Gaze into your baby's eyes, and open yourself to the love you share.

The Head

Before oiling your hands, use your fingertips to make small circular motions all over baby's head.

Let baby know the massage is beginning. Make eye contact; say "hello."

The Legs and Feet

For many babies, the legs are the most pleasurable part of the massage. A toddler may experience growing pains in her legs; these strokes will help ease the discomfort.

The "Milking" strokes aid circulation to the feet and back toward the heart. The "Squeeze and Twist" and "Rolling" strokes help tone and relax the leg muscles.

Massage one leg completely, then the other.

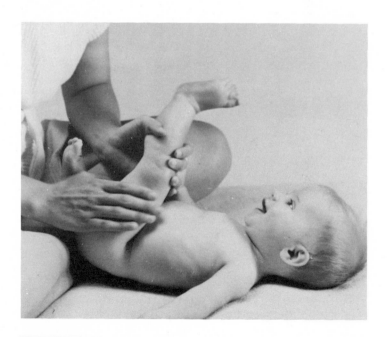

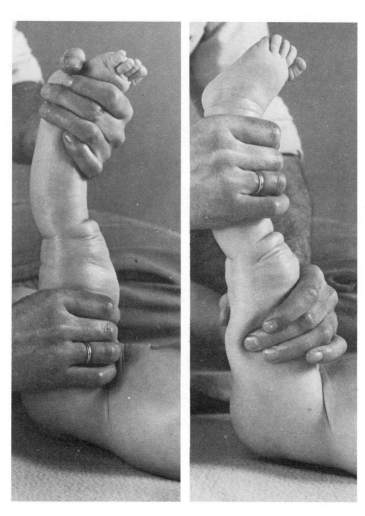

1. *"INDIAN MILKING."* Milk the leg with
the inside edge of each hand, with one following
the other. The outside hand should move
over the buttock; the inside hand should move
inside the crotch and up the leg to the foot.

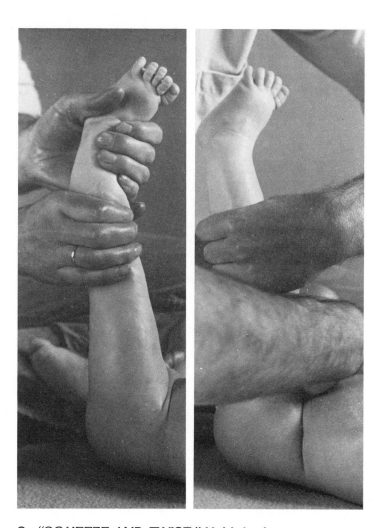

2. *"SQUEEZE AND TWIST."* Hold the leg
as if you were holding a baseball bat. Then
move hands up the leg together, turning
in opposite directions, and squeezing slightly.

There are seventy-two thousand nerve endings in each foot. The many theories on how foot massage works all agree that points on the feet connect with other body areas. Environmental stresses can cause imbalances in our systems which we experience as colds, flu, ear infections, and so forth. Reflexologists (those who study and work with these points on the

3. Push the bottom of the foot from heel to toe with your thumbs, one after another.

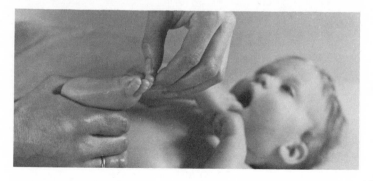

4. Squeeze each toe.

feet) say that by-products of these imbalances, uric acid and excess calcium, crystallize around nerve endings in the feet, blocking the flow of energy through the body. Foot massage, they say, crushes these crystals so that the excess calcium and uric acid are absorbed by the blood and lymph and eventually excreted out of the body.

5. Pull back gently on the balls of the foot.

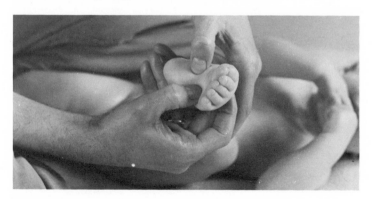

6. Press in with your thumbs all over the bottom of the foot.

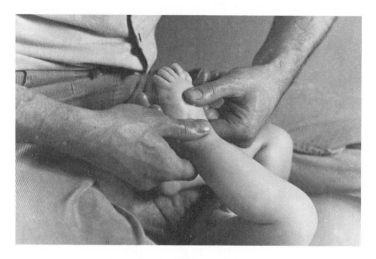

7. Using your thumbs, push the top
of the foot toward the ankle.

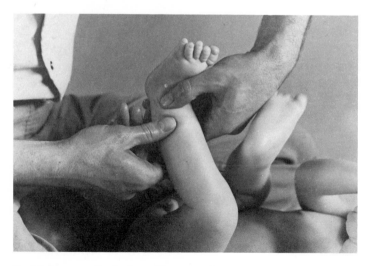

8. Make small circles all around
the ankle with your thumbs.

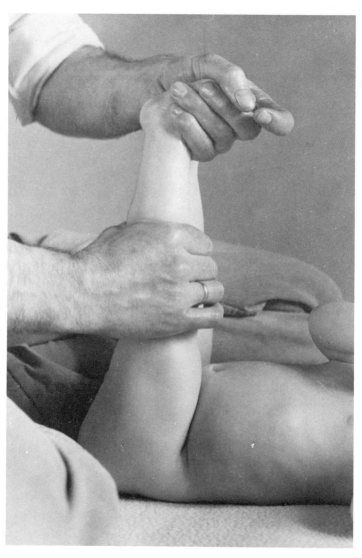

9. *"SWEDISH MILKING."*
Milk the leg from ankle to hip.

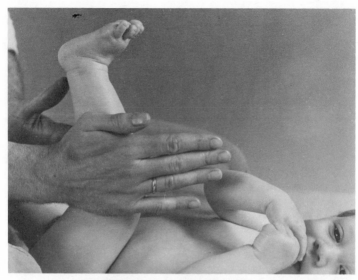

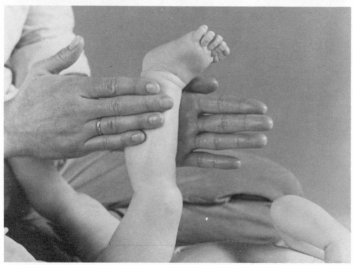

10. *"ROLLING."* Roll the leg
between your hands from knee to ankle.

The Stomach

The strokes for the stomach will tone baby's
intestinal system, and help relieve gas and
constipation. Most of these strokes end at baby's lower
left belly (your right). This is where the eliminative parts
of the intestines are located. The purpose is to move
everything toward the bowel.

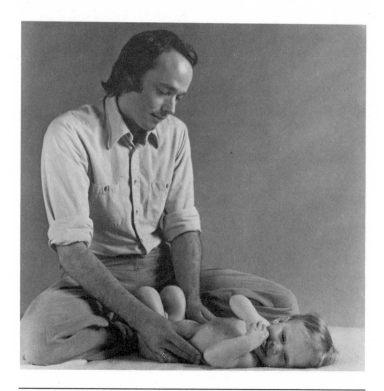

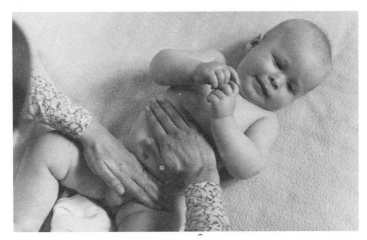

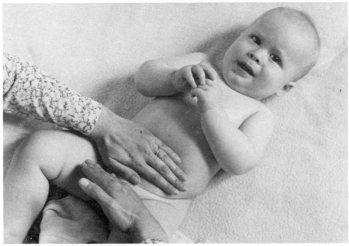

1. "WATER WHEEL."

a. Using the outside of each hand,
make paddling strokes on baby's tummy,
one hand following the other, as if you
were scooping sand toward yourself.

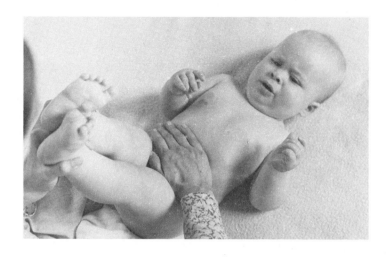

b. Hold up baby's legs with your left hand and grasp the ankles. Then repeat the paddling motion, using the right hand only. This will relax the stomach and will permit you to extend the massaging action a little more deeply.

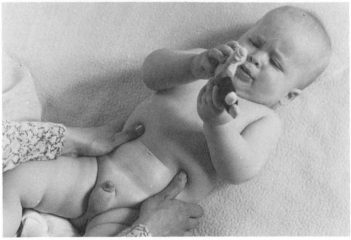

2. With thumbs flat at baby's navel,
push out to the sides. Be sure you use the
flat thumb, and do not poke.

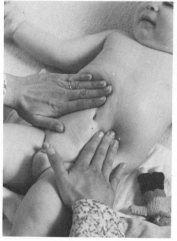
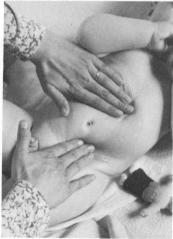

3. *"SUN MOON."* Your right hand
makes an upside-down half-moon from
your left to right. Your left hand makes a
full circle, moving clockwise. While the right
hand is above, the left hand is below.

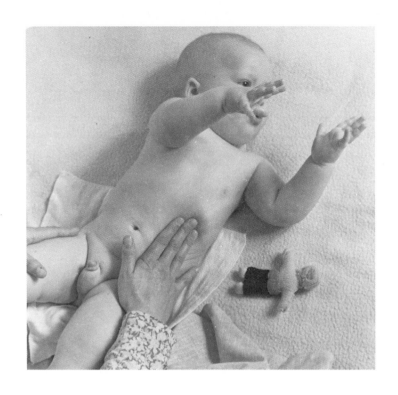

4. *"I LOVE YOU."*

a. Make a single *I*-shaped stroke with your right hand on baby's left belly (your right).

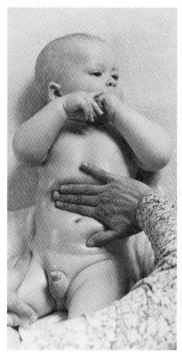 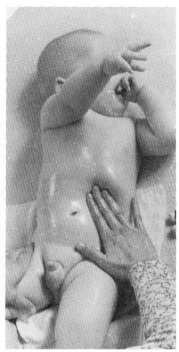

b. *"LOVE."* Make a backward,
sideways *L* going from your left to right.

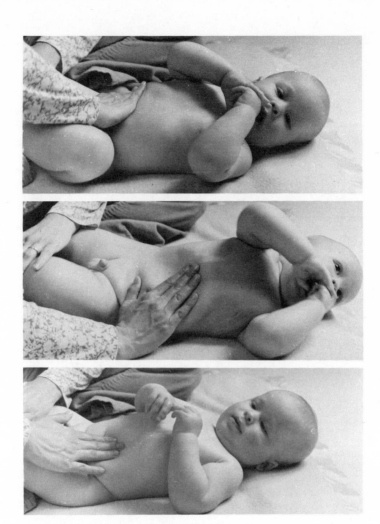

c. *"YOU."* Make an upside-down U,
going from your left to right.

As you go through this series of
motions, say "I love you" in a high-pitched,
cooing tone. Baby will love it!

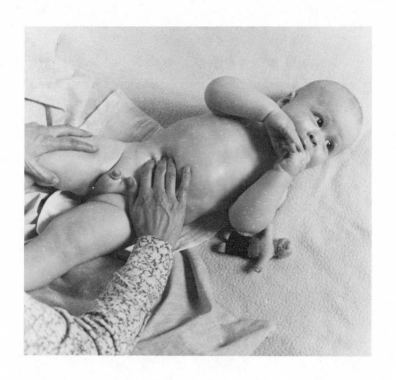

5. *"WALKING."* Using your fingertips,
walk across baby's tummy from your left
to right. You may feel some gas bubbles
moving under your fingers.

The Chest

Massaging the chest will help tone the lungs and the heart. Imagine that you are freeing the baby's breath, and filling his heart with love.

1. *"OPEN BOOK."* With both hands together at the center of the chest, push out to the sides, following the rib cage, as if you were flattening the pages of a book.

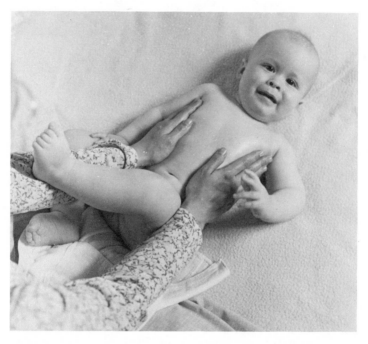

Without lifting the hands from the body, bring them around in a heart-shaped motion to center again.

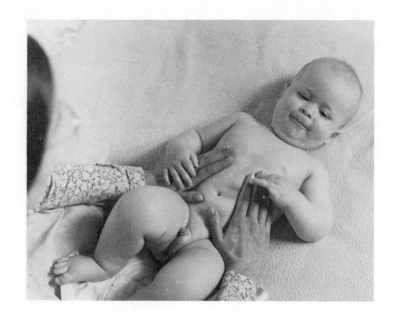

2. *"BUTTERFLY."*

a. To begin this movement,
both hands are at the baby's sides,
at the bottom of the rib cage.

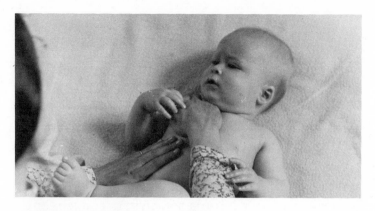

b. The right hand moves across
the chest diagonally, to the baby's right
shoulder; then, pulling gently at the
shoulder, the hand moves down across
the chest and back to its original position.

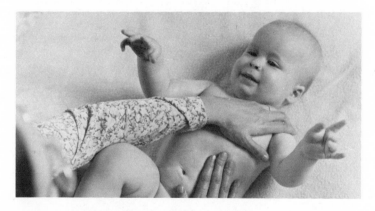

c. Now, the left hand moves across
the chest diagonally, to the baby's left
shoulder, repeating the same motion.
Follow one hand with the other,
rhythmically criss-crossing the chest.

The Arms

In massaging the arms, the complementary differences between Swedish and Indian methods are most strikingly revealed, especially in the "milking" motions.

The traditional Indian way is to "milk" the arm from shoulder to hand, imagining stress and tension leaving the body through the fingertips. The Swedish method is just the opposite, milking from the hand to the shoulder—"toward the heart" for circulation. In using both methods, we combine the Indian concept of balancing and releasing energy with the muscle-toning Swedish massage.

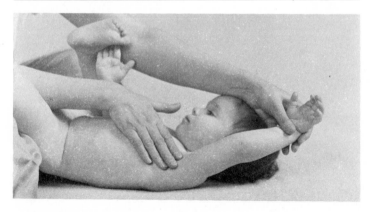

1. *"PITSTOP."* First, lift the arm and stroke the armpit a few times, massaging the important lymph nodes in that area.

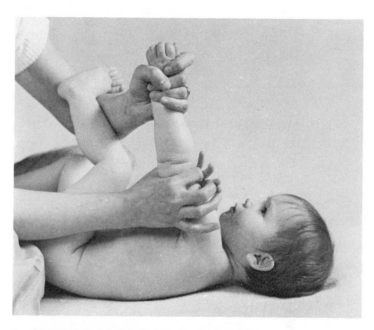

2. *"INDIAN MILKING."* Now, holding
baby's wrist with your left hand, "milk"
the arm with your right hand, starting
at the shoulder and moving to the hand.
Immediately follow with your left hand,
then the right, and so forth. Use the inside
edge of your hand, at the point where the
thumb connects with the index finger.

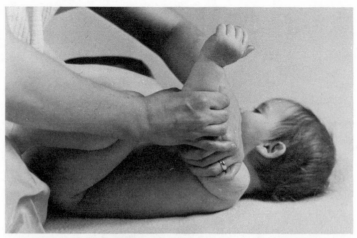

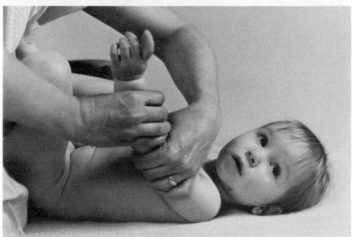

3. *"SQUEEZE AND TWIST."* Hold hands
together around baby's arm at the shoulder
(as if you were holding a baseball bat).
Then move hands in opposite directions,
back and forth, from the shoulder to the
hand, gently squeezing as you do.

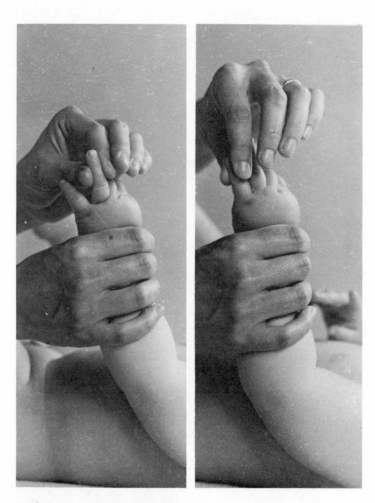

4. Open baby's hand with your thumbs. Roll each tiny finger between your index finger and thumb.

5. Stroke the top of the hand.

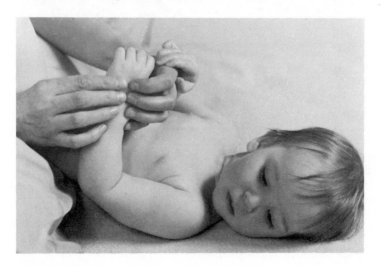

6. Massage the wrist,
making small circles all around.

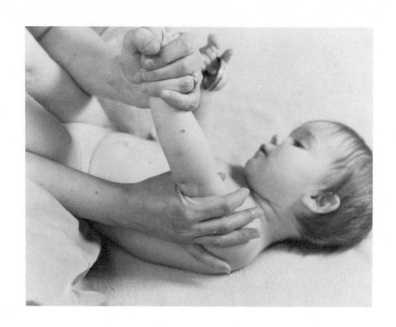

7. *"SWEDISH MILKING."* Milk the
arm from the hand to the shoulder, with
one hand following the other.

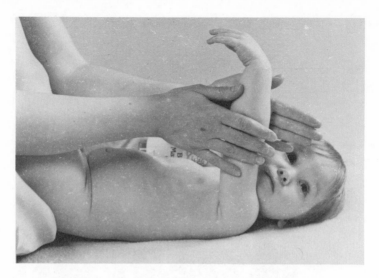

8. *"ROLLING."* Briskly roll baby's arm between your hands from the shoulder to the hand.

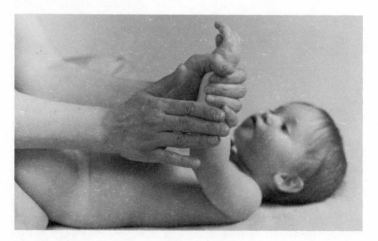

9. To help baby relax his arm, shake it gently and pat it lightly all over.

The Face

Baby's face may accumulate a great deal of tension through sucking, teething, crying and generally interacting with the ever-expanding world around him.

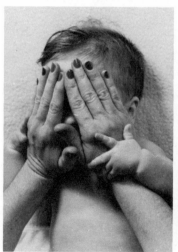

1. With the flats of the fingers, start at the middle of the forehead, and push out to the sides, as if flattening the pages of a book.

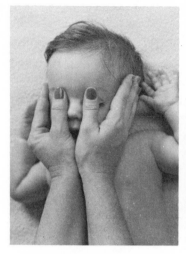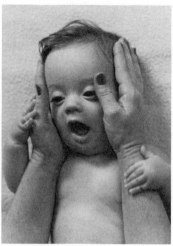

2. With the thumbs, press lightly over the eyes.

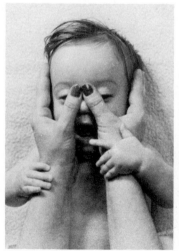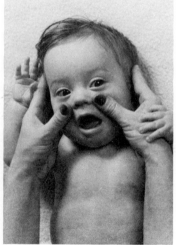

3. With the thumbs, push up on the bridge of the nose, then down across the cheeks.

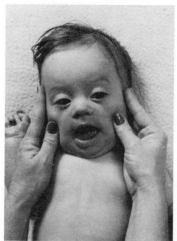

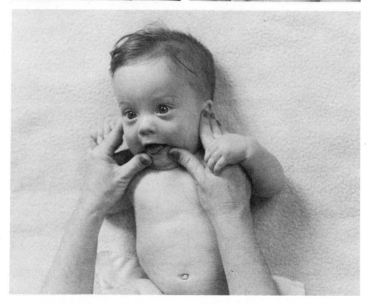

4. With the thumbs, make a smile
on the upper, then the lower lip.

5. Make small circles around the
jaw with your fingertips.

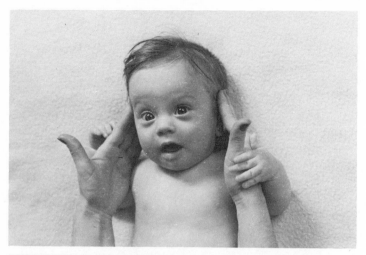

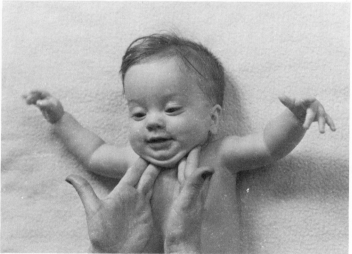

6. Using the fingertips of both hands, go over the ears, around the backs of the ears, and pull up under the chin. This helps relax the jaw and massages important lymph nodes in this area.

The Back

The back is often a favorite with babies and toddlers alike. It is the most relaxing part of the massage. These strokes also act as a kind of "warm-up" for the exercises which follow.

To massage the back, turn baby on his tummy, either on the floor, or on your lap with your legs outstretched.

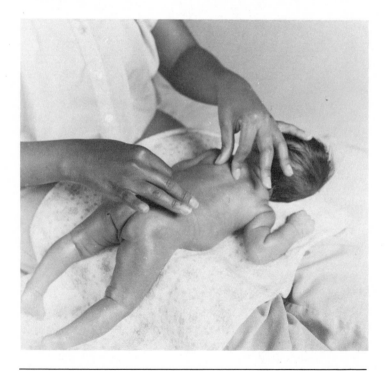

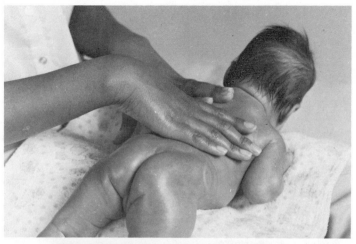

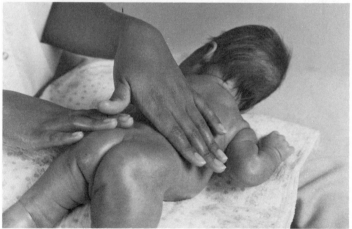

1. *"BACK AND FORTH."* Start with
both hands together at the top of the back,
at right angles to the spine. Move your hands
back and forth, in opposite directions, going
down the back to the buttocks, then up
the shoulders, and back down once again.

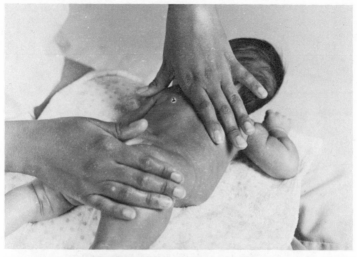

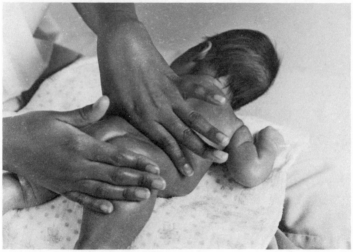

2. Keep the right hand stationary at the buttocks. Then, beginning at the neck, the left hand swoops down to meet the right hand at the buttocks.

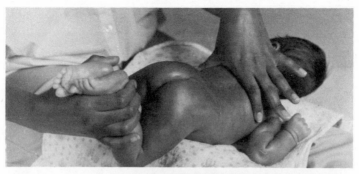

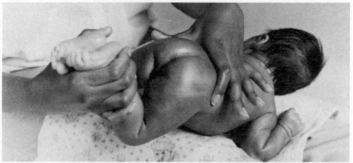

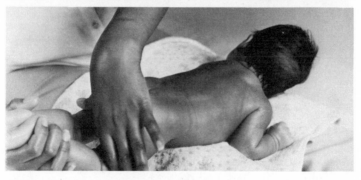

3. Hold up the legs with your right
hand. Your left hand will then repeat the
"swooping" motion, this time moving
all the way down the legs to the ankles.

As baby grows, you can feel muscles develop right under your fingertips!

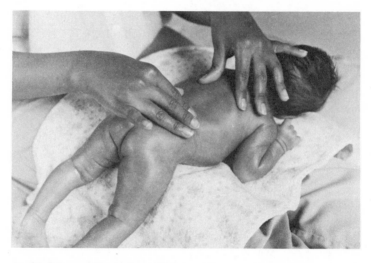

4. Make small circles all around the back with your fingertips.

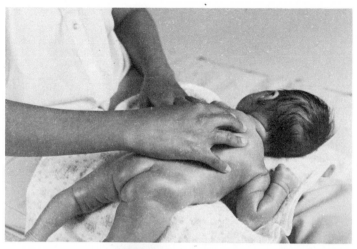

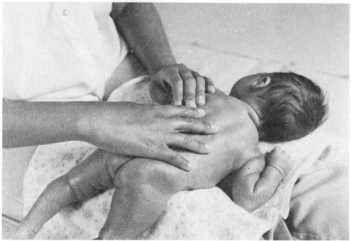

5. With the right hand open and
fingers spread apart, the fingers "comb"
the back, starting at the neck and moving to
the buttocks. Each stroke will be progressively
lighter, ending with a "feather touch."

Gentle Exercises

These exercises are simple movements that gently stretch baby's arms and legs, massage his stomach and pelvis, and align his spine. Repeat four or five times.

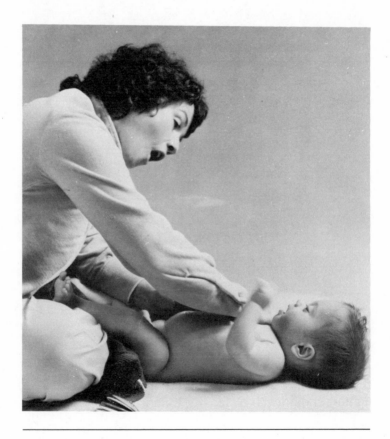

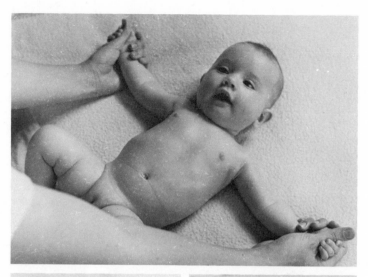

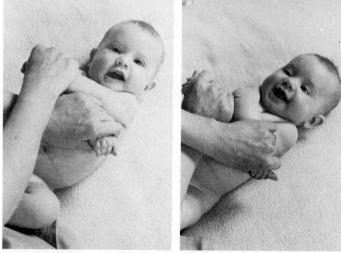

1. Holding baby's arms at the
wrist, stretch them out to the sides,
then cross them at his chest twice.

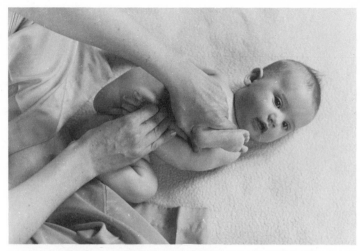

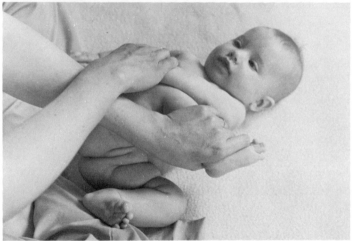

2. Hold one arm at the wrist, and the
opposite leg at the ankle. Gently bring the arm
down to the crotch and the foot up toward
the shoulder, then cross the leg and arm

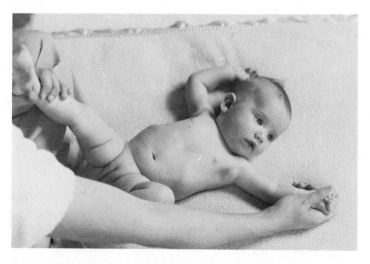

so that the arm goes to the outside of the leg.
Now stretch them out in opposite directions.
Repeat with opposite arm and leg. Note:
With an older child, bring the knee, rather
than the foot, up to cross with the arm.

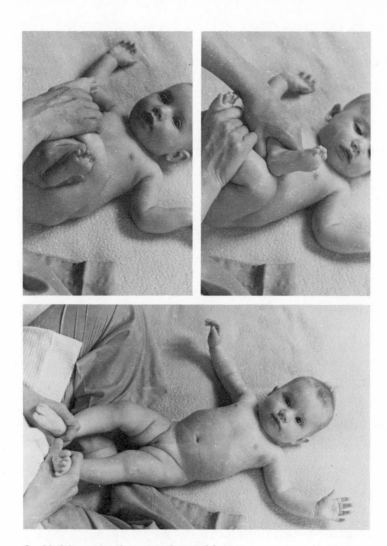

3. Holding the legs at the ankles.
cross them at the stomach four times,
then stretch them out straight.

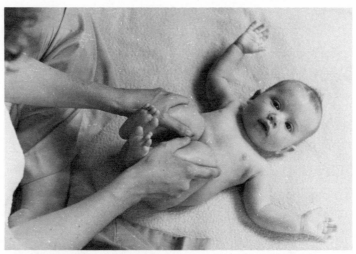

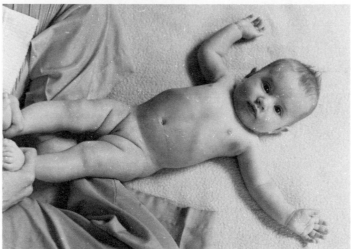

4. Push the knees together up into
the tummy, then stretch them out straight.
If baby resists straightening his legs, shake
them gently and encourage him to relax.

Review of the Strokes

1. Small circles around head.

2. Oil hands.

3. Legs and feet:
   a. Indian Milking
   b. Squeeze and Twist
   c. Push sole of foot
   d. Squeeze each toe
   e. Pull back at balls of foot
   f. Press in all over bottom of foot
   g. Over top of foot toward ankle
   h. Small circles around ankle
   i. Swedish Milking
   j. Rolling

4. Stomach:
   a. Water Wheel
   b. Water Wheel with legs up
   c. Thumbs to sides
   d. Sun Moon
   e. I Love You
   f. Walking

5. Chest:

   a. Open Book
   b. Butterfly

6. Arms and Hands:

   a. Pitstop
   b. Indian Milking
   c. Squeeze and Twist
   d. Open hand
   e. Roll each finger
   f. Top of hand
   g. Small circles around wrist
   h. Swedish Milking
   i. Rolling

7. Face:

   a. Open Book
   b. Thumbs over eyes
   c. Push up on bridge of nose, down across cheek
   d. Smile on upper and lower lip
   e. Small circles around jaw
   f. Over ears and under chin

8. Back:

   a. Back and Forth
   b. Swooping to bottom
   c. Swooping to ankles
   d. Small circles all over back
   e. Comb back

9. Gentle Exercises:

   a. Cross arms

b. Cross arm and leg
c. Cross legs
d. Legs up and down
e. Legs up and down alternating

10. *And a Kiss to Grow On!*

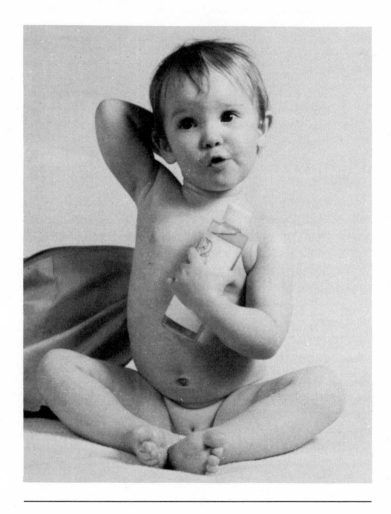

ABBREVIATED MASSAGE

Sometimes you want to give baby a quick rubdown on the run, when changing diapers, or just before bed. Here is an abbreviated massage that will take only a few minutes but will still provide the benefits of communication and relaxation your baby needs.

This massage can be done with or without oil or lotion.

1. Circles around head
2. Open Book on forehead
3. Circles on jaw
4. Open Book on chest
5. Roll arms, open hands
6. Sun Moon on stomach
7. Roll legs
8. Soles of feet
9. Back and Forth on back
10. Comb back

Fussing and Tension

This is my sad time of day.
—ARNOLD LOBEL

At this point, you may be imaging yourself lovingly massaging your baby, as she lies there contentedly listening to your voice, gazing into your eyes, and perhaps, even falling asleep. This will probably happen quite often, and when it does, it's wonderful! But it is also true that most babies will fuss or cry at times during their massage. If you understand the reasons for baby's fussiness, you will be much more comfortable and more knowledgeable in the best ways to help her.

Infants grow so rapidly it is small wonder there is often so much tension in their little bodies. They are working so hard to develop muscle coordination, that it is logical they may occasionally ache and feel out of sorts.

When *your* body aches, a massage feels both

good and painful at the same time. Your muscles are sore, and even a gentle touch can be uncomfortable. Still, being touched feels so good and relaxing, it's hard to tell if your grunts and grimaces are from pain or pleasure. Often a massage can remind you of aches you never knew you had; but afterward the feeling of relief and release you experience is well worth the temporary discomfort you've endured.

Massage is another new experience for your little one. At first, she may react negatively to the sensations that she is experiencing; but after she becomes accustomed to being touched in this fashion, she will begin to enjoy the routine. So take it easy at first, and acquaint her with these new sensations slowly.

Throughout the first year, babies seem to be tense and/or sore in various parts of their bodies. In the first three months, your infant may hold her arms closely to her body and protest loudly if you try to massage or straighten them. Observing her closely, you will see how hard she is working to strengthen and coordinate her arms. Since she has held them near her for months in the womb, having them pulled on may be a downright scary feeling. If your baby seems to cry especially hard when you massage her arms, you may want to leave them for last, using just the gentle shaking and patting movements described in "Helping Baby Learn to Relax."

Show her that it is "okay" to open and relax her arms. Touch her arms in an especially gentle and loving fashion. As she begins to outgrow this stage, you can start using firmer strokes. By paying attention to her arms at this stage, you are beginning to teach her how to relax her own body. She will probably enjoy the back massage most at this time, and this feeling will, in turn, help her to relax her arms.

From four to seven months, soreness and tension may move into the back, as baby begins to sit and crawl. Her face may be another sensitive spot due to the crying, sucking and teething described in facial exercises (page 79). If so, simply use gentle touching, stroking, and kissing when you get a negative reaction to any firmer touch. During this "trimester," the leg massage will probably be the most enjoyed portion of your routine.

Toward the end of the first year, the tension may move into the legs as baby learns to stand and walk. This can be an especially trying time for some babies, who will steadfastly refuse to be massaged at all. Every bit of their attention will be focused on walking and teething. They may be very fussy and short-tempered until they have mastered the art of walking and have most of their teeth. Then they will slow down a little, having accomplished gargantuan feats during their first year of life.

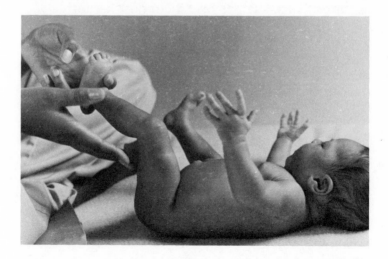

If they have been massaged regularly from infancy onward, they will probably begin to enjoy their massage more than ever before. They will giggle and sing with you, and help by massaging themselves. And, by 1½, you may find your little one very seriously massaging her teddy bear. Before you know it, she is massaging you! Ah, the universal law of action and reaction—what you do ultimately comes full circle back to you!

Here are some things you can do if baby cries or fusses while being massaged:

1. Breathe deeply and make every effort to relax. Then allow baby to fuss a little. Often she will release the tension during the massage and be a lot happier, more relaxed, and sleep more soundly the rest of the time. A mother in one of my classes had a very "colicky" tense baby, who completely changed after being massaged daily for a week. This mother reported that though the baby cried loudly during the massage, she was very happy and relaxed during the rest of the day—much to the comfort and relief of the entire family.

2. Give baby a short break in the middle of the massage to nurse, cuddle, or walk a little. If she seems to enjoy the massage at first, and then becomes restless, try shortening the time—massaging one part of the body each day, instead of all at once.

3. Give baby a small toy or teether to play with and chew on.

4. Once again, breathe deeply and relax yourself. In many ways, we are like mirrors for our children. If they look at us and see calm, they will try to reflect this same attitude back to us.

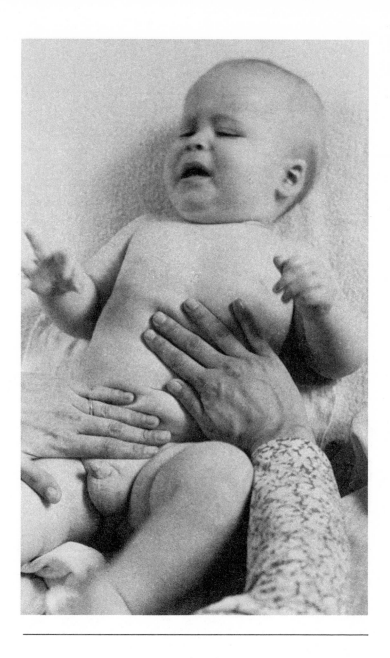

When Baby Is Ill

Can a mother sit and hear
An infant groan, an infant fear?
No, no! never can it be!
Never, never can it be!
                    —WILLIAM BLAKE

I n times of illness, a massage not only can be
comforting, but can also help relieve such painful
symptoms as aches, fever, and congestion. Of
course, as is the case with any significant deviation
from health in your baby, you should consult your
doctor first.

To help bring down a high fever, you may use
some of the same motions as in the basic massage.
Use *warm water* on your hands instead of oil, and
keep baby's body covered, except the part you're
working on. Working from the chest to the extremities,
dip your hand in the water, then briskly rub the body.
The idea is to bring the heat up to the surface of the
skin, where the water will evaporate and help cool it.

You can use a similar technique on your baby to

help ease chest congestion. First, do the regular massage motions for the chest, using oil on your hands. (A little eucalyptus or Mentholatum may also help.) Then, tip the baby at an angle with his head down. Using a small cup (the clean plastic cap from a bottle of fabric softener works nicely) or something with a small rim, press in and pull out gently all over the chest and back. The gentle suction helps pull mucus away from the lungs so it can be coughed up. A vaporizer in baby's room will help, too.

For nasal congestion, assemble the following: a nasal aspirator, a dropper, a handkerchief, and a cup of warm salted water (ratio: ½ tsp. salt per cup of warm water). Do the massage motions for the face, especially the ones for the sinus area, to help relax the area and loosen mucus. Then place a drop of the warm salted water in each nostril, and suction out the mucus with the aspirator, blowing it into the handkerchief after each time. The warm salt water is easy on baby's nose and helps loosen the mucus considerably. Baby will not enjoy this process, but it may be necessary if his stuffiness is preventing him from being able to suck.

GAS AND "COLIC"

There has been much speculation over the years concerning "colic" (or constant crying and irritability) and its causes. Some people think it is due to gastrointestinal problems, and others think it may be environmental stress and tension to which a baby is particularly sensitive. Whatever the cause, a constantly crying baby is difficult and even traumatic for any parent to handle. I have found that massage is one way that a parent can attempt to help baby through these trying times, often with a great deal of success.

Sometimes a baby's gastrointestinal system is slow in achieving top functioning capacity. In the meantime, painful gas and constipation can be a problem. If baby is stiff and seems to be in pain when he is crying, he may have gas. Here are a couple of suggestions that may help to relieve it.

First, study the strokes for the tummy area. Strokes that are most helpful for gas are "Water Wheel" and "Sun Moon." Do "Water Wheel" six times, with one hand following the other. Then push baby's knees up firmly into his tummy, hold for a few seconds, and then pull them out straight. Now, repeat the same process, this time using the "Sun Moon" technique. Next, do "Water Wheel" once more, and again push the knees into the tummy and hold. If no gas is released, wait awhile and try again.

In the meantime, there are some other things you can do that may help. Take baby into a warm bath. The warmth and comfort of the water may help him to relax and move the gas. Take baby's temperature rectally. The gentle stimulation of the thermometer will sometimes remind his lower intestine to do its job. A back massage is also good for this problem.

It isn't easy to see your little one in such distress, and it is terribly trying on your nerves. But it is comforting to know that you have on hand a series of procedures that may help to greatly ease his difficulties.

THE PREMATURE BABY

Premature babies and their parents usually undergo quite a long and difficult period of hospitalization and posthospital adjustments. Though your premature baby is tiny, he can be massaged. In fact, your touch can be very therapeutic, and will help you feel closer to your baby.

Before your baby is discharged from the hospital, you can begin with simple, gentle strokes. Gently massage his brow or his legs with your fingertips, cup your hand around his head, sing, and talk to him. Though the equipment on hand can be intimidating, you are the most important person to your baby; don't be afraid to touch him—he needs you.

When your baby comes home, you can begin a daily massage routine. In the first month or so, massage only his back and legs, using gentle strokes with your fingertips. Use the relaxation techniques (page 25) more than anything else during this period. He needs to know how to relax, and to begin to associate touch with pleasure. The massage should be very short in the beginning—only about five minutes—and the massage area should be very comfortable and warm. Sit on the floor or bed with your back against a wall and your knees up. Place the baby on a towel-covered pillow in your lap, leaning up against your thighs. This brings the baby closer to your face, and the pillow will give him a feeling of support and warmth. When you massage his back, turn him on his side, supporting his chest with one hand as you gently massage with the other. The "formal" strokes shown in this book can wait until he is bigger and more comfortable when you touch him.

You will find massage a lovely way to communicate with your baby, and to help him grow strong and healthy. The engaging young man who was our model for the facial strokes (pages 79–83) was a premature baby who is now an active kindergartener. Jonah's bright eyes and sweet disposition are remarkable testimony to the saying, "Small is beautiful"!

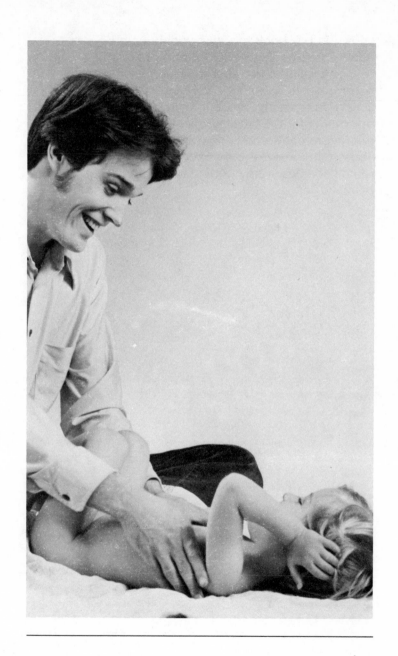

The Older Child

The plants' bright blessing springs forth
From earth's gentle being,
And human children rise up
With grateful hearts to join
The spirits of the world.

—RUDOLPH STEINER

T he child who has been regularly massaged from
infancy will continue to enjoy it as she grows.
Leg and back cramps that often accompany
growth spurts will be pleasantly relieved with a
massage.

Bonding between parents and child
continues—and, just because a child has graduated
from the "in-arms" stage doesn't mean she no longer
needs your loving touch. She will no longer be nursing,
she won't cuddle in the same way, her circle of
support will widen, and she will be increasingly busy
exploring the infinite possibilities of her world. But even
as she grows out of her mother's and father's arms,
she will come to cherish those moments of closeness

that reassure her that Mommy and Daddy are always there with a warm smile and a loving massage.

Though sometime in the first nine months is the ideal time to start, it is never too late to begin the massage routine. Usually, a child between one and three or four years of age who has not been massaged from infancy will be much too busy to be still, but you may be able to start with a short, gentle back massage at bedtime, without protest. Once the child becomes accustomed to being massaged, she, herself, will begin asking for it.

STROKE AND
EXERCISE MODIFICATION

For older babies (crawling and up) some of the massage techniques must be varied somewhat to accommodate for the lengthening of their limbs.

Legs: The "Milking" stroke should be done in two parts; thigh, then shin. "Squeeze and Twist" and "Rolling" should start just below the knee rather than at the hip.

Arms: The "Milking" strokes should be done in two parts; upper, then lower arm. "Squeeze and Twist" and "Rolling" can begin at the elbow.

Exercises: When the leg and arm are crossed diagonally, bend the leg and cross the knee (rather than the foot) with the arm. Eliminate the leg-crossing exercise.

If your child is over one year of age, you can eliminate the exercises from the massage routine. She

has many opportunities to stretch and exercise her
limbs and back in the course of her busy day.

RHYMES AND GAMES
FOR THE OLDER BABY

Working with an older child requires a slightly
different approach than does massaging the tiny baby.
To keep the child interested and involved, you may

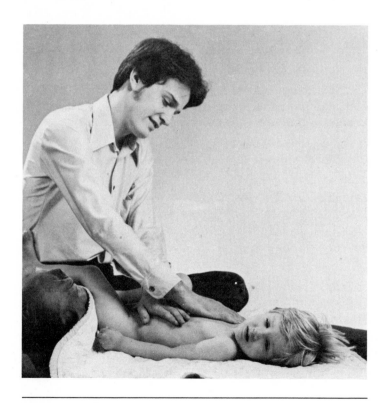

want to vary the massage each time, adding "zip" by means of stories, songs, and animation on your part. For instance, one of the tummy strokes most enjoyed by older children is "I Love You" (see page 64). They enjoy chiming in with you as you stretch the words out, cooing in a sing-song voice. When you massage the feet, you can play "This little piggy went to market." Little games, songs, and stories that you invent as you massage your little one will involve her, entertain her active mind, and promote the kind of communication that stimulates and utilizes all of her developing senses.

FEET AND TOES

This little piggy went to market
This little piggy stayed home
This little piggy had roast beef (tofu? pomegranates?)
This little piggy had none
This little piggy went wee wee wee wee all the way
　　home.

One is a lady that sits in the sun;
Two is a baby and three is a nun;
Four is a lily with innocent breast;
Five is a birdie asleep in the nest.

This little piggy got into the barn,
This one ate all the corn.
This one said he wasn't well,
This one said he'd go and tell,
And this one said—squeak, squeak, squeak!
I can't get over the barn door sill.

See saw, Marjorie Daw,
The hen flew over the barn.
She counted her baby chicks one by one,
    (count each toe except the baby toe)
But she couldn't find the little white one.
Here it is, here it is, here it is!

(Start with the little toe.)

This little cow eats grass,
This little cow eats hay,
This little cow looks over the hedge,
This little cow runs away,
And this BIG cow does nothing at all
But lie in the fields all day!
We'll chase her, and chase her,
and CHASE her!

(This rhyme goes well with the foot strokes;
see numbers 5 and 6, page 55.)

Pitty patty polt,
Shoe the wild colt.
Here's a nail,
There's a nail,
Pitty patty polt!

TUMMY

(See Sun-Moon stroke, number 3, page 63.)

Round and round the garden
Went the teddy bear,
One step, two step, tickley under there!
    (walk fingers up to armpit)

FINGERS

Five little fishes swimming in a pool
    (open hand)
First one said, "The pool is cool"
Second one said, "The pool is deep"
Third one said, "I want to sleep"
Fourth one said, "Let's dive and dip"
Fifth one said, "I spy a ship"
They all jumped up and went ker'splash
    (stroke top of hand)
Away the five little fishes dash
    (shake hand to relax)

(Begin with thumb.)

This is the father, short and stout
This is the mother, with children all about
This is the brother, tall you see
This is the sister with dolly on her knee
This is the baby, sure to grow
And here is the family, all in a row.

Here is a tree with leaves so green
Here are the apples that hang between
    *(hold thumb and small finger and wiggle three
    middle fingers)*
When the wind blows the apples fall
    (hold baby's wrist and gently shake)
And here is a basket to gather them all.
    (cup baby's hand in yours)

Five little kittens
All black and white
    (cup baby's fist in your hands)
Sleeping soundly

All through the night
Meow, meow, meow, meow, meow
        (raise each finger)
It's time to get up now!

Within a little apple
So cosy and so small
There are five little chambers
        (cup baby's fist in your hands)
Around a little hall.

In every room are sleeping
Two seeds of golden brown
They're lying there and dreaming
        (open each finger and peek in)
In beds of eiderdown

They're dreaming there of sunshine
And how it's going to be
        (stroke top of hand)
When they shall hang as apples
Upon a Christmas tree.
        (hold baby's wrist and gently shake)

FACE

(See pages 79–83 for strokes.)

Knock knock
        (Open Book stroke on forehead)
Peek in
        (over eyes with thumbs)
Open the latch
        *(up on nose and down across cheek with
        thumbs)*
And walk right in
        (thumbs over mouth)

Hello, Mr. Chinny-chin-chin!
(gently wiggle chin)

Two little eyes to look around
Two little ears to hear each sound
One little nose to smell what's sweet
One little mouth that likes to eat

Peek-a-boo, I see you
Hiding behind the chair
Peek-a-boo, I see you
Hiding there.

GAMES TO PLAY WITH EXERCISES

ARMS

Up so high
(stretch arms up)
Down so low
(bring arms down)
Give a little shake
(shake hands at wrists)
And hold them so
(put hands together)

This is my right arm, hold it flat
(hold arm out flat)
This is my left arm, just like that
Right arm, left arm, hug myself
(cross arms on chest)
Left arm, right arm,
(uncross and hold flat again)
Catch a little elf!
*(bring hands together quickly, then ask, "Did
you catch him?" and peek in cupped hands)*

Pat-a-cake, pat-a-cake
  (pat baby's hands together)
Baker man
Bake me a cake
As fast as you can.
Roll it, and pat it
  (roll hands around each other, and pat one with the other)
And mark it with a *B*
And put it in the oven
  (hold arms up, then down, and point to baby and self)
For baby and me.

LEGS

One leg, two legs
  (cross over tummy)
Hot cross buns
Right leg, left leg
  (pull out flat)
Isn't that fun?
  (gently shake)

Up
  (knees into tummy)
Down
  (pull out straight)
Up, down
Up, down
And shake them all around.

HELPING AN OLDER CHILD
ADJUST TO A NEW BABY

Through the house what busy joy,
Just because the infant boy
Has a tiny tooth to show.
I have got a double row,
All as white, and all as small;
Yet no one cares for mine at all.
                    —MARY LAMB

A new baby is a fascinating, fearful creature to his
older brother or sister. Hovered over and protected by
adults, the baby seems to be an unapproachable,
somehow dangerous little being. Much has been
written on the importance of letting your older child
know that he is still loved and cherished in his own
right when a new baby comes into the family. The next
step is to help the older child and the baby to begin a
relationship of their own. It usually takes quite a bit
longer for a child to fully "bond" with a new sibling.
His first task is to understand that the baby is "here,"
that mother is all right, that he is still loved as much as
before, and that life goes on.

As you massage your baby every day, your older
child will occasionally observe. He may remember
being massaged (in fact he may still enjoy being
massaged) and identify with the baby. They share an
experience, have something in common.

If your child is given the opportunity to massage
the baby occasionally (only if he wants to, of course),
he will benefit by it in many ways, as will baby. The

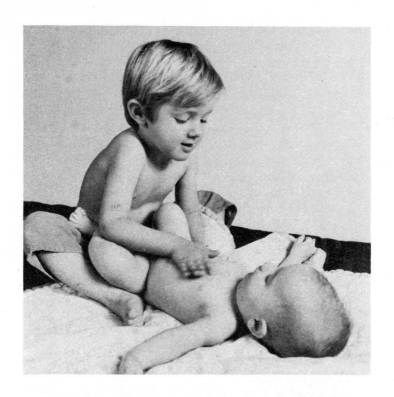

older child will bond with the baby in the same ways that you do—with eye contact, touch, movement, sound. He will learn that baby is not necessarily so dangerous and fragile, but a person like himself. His confidence will bloom as he comes to realize his own competence as a caretaker and protector. The baby will respond to him, overcoming her initial fear of his sometimes clumsy, rough handling or startling behavior. She will begin to relate to him as a loving peer and ally.

It is best to delay suggesting that an older child massage the new baby until the baby has passed that stage of fragility when she is easily startled. Usually three or four months of age is about the right time, though a little earlier may be appropriate for an older child who is over four. Don't worry about the method or whether or not the child uses oil. You can show him a couple of things (the "Open Book" stroke on the chest is best, see page 68) and then let him do it as he pleases. He will at first be hesitant and may need your encouragement to touch the baby. He will probably stroke the baby only a couple of times. But even the tiniest amount of contact will be very beneficial. Be sure to express your pleasure and pride to your child; let him know that he did a good job and that his massaging is valuable to the baby.

References

Ainsworth, M. *Infancy in Uganda.* Baltimore, Md.: The Johns Hopkins University Press, 1967.

Ambuel, J., and Harris, B. "Failure to Thrive: A Study of Failure to Grow in Height and Weight." Ohio Medical Journal, no. 59 (1963).

Altmann, M. *Maternal Behavior in Mammals.* New York: John Wiley & Sons, Inc., 1963.

Barnett, C. R., Leiderman, P. H., Grobstein, R., and Klaus, M. H. "Neonatal Separation: The Maternal Side of Interactional Deprivation." Pediatrics, no. 45 (1970).

Berkson, Devaki. *The Foot Book.* New York: Funk & Wagnalls, Inc., 1977.

Bowlby, J. *Attachment and Loss.* New York: Basic Books, Inc., Publishers, 1969.

Brazelton, T. B. "Effect of Maternal Expectations on Early Infant Behavior." Early Child Development Care, no. 2 (1973).

_____. "Importance of Behavioral Assessment of the Neonate. Current Problems in Pediatrics." December 1976.

Briggs, D. *Your Child's Self Esteem.* Garden City, New York: Doubleday & Company, Inc., 1975.

Carpenter, E. *Eskimo Realities.* New York: Holt, Rinehart and Winston, 1973.

Cass-Beggs, B. *Your Baby Needs Music.* New York: St. Martin's Press, Inc., 1978.

Condon, W. S., and Sander, L. W. "Neonate Movement Is Synchronized with Adult Speech: Interactional Participation and Language Acquisition." Science, no. 183 (1974).

Crelin, E. *Functional Anatomy of the Newborn.* New Haven, Conn.: Yale University Press, 1973.

Daikin, L. *The Lullaby Book*. London: Publications, Ltd., 1959.

Davis, A. *Let's Have Healthy Children*. New York: Harcourt Brace Jovanovich, 1972.

Dunn, J. *Distress and Comfort.* The Developing Child Series. Cambridge, Mass.: Harvard University Press, 1977.

Eisenberg, et al. "Auditory Behavior in the Human Neonate." Journal of Speech and Hearing Research, no. 7 (1964).

Elmer E., and Gregg, G. S. "Developmental Characteristics of Abused Children." Pediatrics, no. 40 (1967).

Geestesleven, U. *Clump-a-Dump and Snickle-Snack, Pentatonic Songs for Children*. Spring Valley, New York: Mercury Press, 1966.

Glas, N. *Conception, Birth and Early Childhood*. Spring Valley, New York: Anthroposophic Press, no date.

Harlow, H. F., Harlow, M. K., and Hansen, E. W. *Maternal Behavior in Mammals*. New York: John Wiley & Sons, Inc., 1963.

The Holistic Health Handbook. Berkeley, Calif.: Berkeley Holistic Health Center, 1978.

Keker, D. *Building Positive Self-Concepts*. Minneapolis, Minn.: Burgess Publishing Company, 1974.

Klaus, M. H., and Kennell, J. H. *Maternal Infant Bonding*. St. Louis, Mo.: C.V. Mosby Company, 1976.

Klaus, M. H., et al. *Maternal Attachment and Mothering Disorders: A Round Table*. Skillman, N. J., Johnson and Johnson, 1975.

Klaus, M. H., Jerauld, R., Kreger, N., McAlpine, W., Steffa, M., and Kennell, J. H. "Maternal Attachment: Importance of the First Post Partum Days." New England Journal of Medicine, no. 286 (1972).

Kramer, L., and Pierpont, M. "Rocking Waterbeds and Auditory Stimuli to Enhance Growth of Preterm Infants." Journal of Pediatrics, no. 88 (1976).

Matterson, E. *This Little Puffin*. London: Penguin Books, 1972.

Medvin, J. *Prenatal Yoga and Natural Birth*. Albion, Calif.: Freestone Publishing Company, 1974.

Montagu, A. *Touching*. New York: Harper & Row Publishers, 1971.

Neurnberger, P. *Freedom from Stress*. Honesdale, Pa.: Himalayan Institute, 1981.

Opie, I., and Opie, P. *The Oxford Nursery Rhyme Book.* London: Oxford University Press, 1955.

Osofsky, J. *Handbook of Infant Development.* New York: John Wiley & Sons, Inc., 1979.

Pearce, J. *Magical Child.* New York: E. P. Dutton & Co., Inc., 1977.

Powell, L. F. "The Effect of Extra Stimulation and Maternal Involvement on the Development of Low Birthweight Infants and on Maternal Behavior." Child Review, no. 45 (1974).

The Parenting Advisor. Princeton Center for Infancy. Garden City, New York: Anchor Press/Doubleday & Company, Inc., 1977.

Queen, S., and Habenstein, R. *The Family in Various Cultures.* New York: J. B. Lippincott Company, 1961.

Samuels, M., and Samuels, N. *The Well Baby Book.* New York: Simon & Schuster, Inc., 1979.

Schaffer, R. *Mothering.* The Developing Child Series. Cambridge, Mass.: Harvard University Press, 1977.

Sinclair, D. *Human Growth after Birth.* New York: Oxford University Press, Inc., Oxford Medical Publications, 1969.

Tanner, J. M., and Taylor, G. R. *Growth.* New York: Time Life Books, 1973.

Teaching Asanas: An Ananda Marga Manual for Teachers. Los Altos Hills, Calif.: Amrit Publications, 1973.

Trause, M. A., Hale, D., and Kennell, M. H. "How Early Is Early Contact? Defining the Limits of the Sensitive Period." Pediatric Research, no. 10 (1976).

Trotter, S. and Thoman, E. B. "The Social Responsiveness of Infants." Johnson and Johnson, 1978.

Wolff, P. "The Causes, Controls, and Organization of Behavior in the Neonate." Monograph 17. Psychological Issues, vol. V, no. 1 (1965).

Zarrow, M. X., Gandelman, R., and Renenberg, V. "Prolactin: Is It an Essential Hormone for Maternal Behavior in the Mammal?" Hormones Behavior, no. 2 (1971).

Zborowsky, M., and Herzog, E. *Life Is with People.* New York: International University Press, 1952.

ABOUT THE AUTHOR

After graduating from college in 1972, Vimala Schneider participated in a training program for yoga instructors and travelled to India to study. It was there that she learned the traditional Indian baby massage from rural mothers in Bihar. During her first pregnancy in 1976, she began an intensive course of study which encompassed childbirth, infant development, Indian and Swedish methods of massage, and maternal bonding. After the birth of her son, Narayana, Vimala developed the infant massage program. She also helped found the Caesarean Birth Education Group, designed and conducted a training program for Caesarean support counsellors, and started the parents' support section of the organization.

Vimala gave birth to her second child, a daughter, Sadhana, in 1978. She continues to teach infant massage in Denver, and has developed an instructor training program to make her course available throughout the United States. Vimala teaches yoga and meditation through Ananda Marga, a service organization with which she has been active for over ten years, and is the author of *Beginning Meditation: An Introduction to Ananda Marga.*

Family-Time Discoveries

All Natural Baby Massage Oil with Vitamin E

A beneficial oil. Cold-pressed from fruits, seeds and nuts. No mineral oil or petroleum derivative. Safe even when baby chews on fist. 8 oz. unbreakable bottle **$3.00**

All Natural Baby Powder

Contains only aloe vera, cornstarch and zinc oxide. Healing, cooling – protects and soothes. Perfect for use by every member of the family. 5 oz. unbreakable bottle with shaker top. **$3.00**

Family-Time Inflatable Bye-Bye Beds

Take along for car, van or RV – camping, overnight at grandma's house. Inflates in a second with hand pump, hair dryer or by mouth. Textured vinyl cover. Tubular air cell support system. With matching carrying tote. Twin size **$29.95** Full size **$39.95**
Add $4.95 shipping & handling

Double-Duty Nikki Chair/Stool

Rugged – sturdy – steady. Perfect for baby. Beautifully crafted in ash wood. Carefully constructed so as not to tip. Top flips down to provide a step stool Natural wood – hand rubbed oil finish. All assembled.

Personalized* (print baby's name on separate piece of paper – maximum of 10 letters) Measures 11-1/2" wide x 12-1/2" high x 10" deep. Seat is 7" wide. Weighs 3-3/4 lbs.
*No extra charge for personalizing. **$19.95**
Shipping & handling $2.50

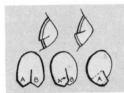

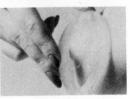

Contoured Disposable Nursing Pads

A uniquely designed pad that offers triple thick air-fluff layers for super absorbency. 100% paper product that can adjust to any milk flow. Fits all bra cups. Pack of 48 pads.

$4.50

Convertible Breast Pump / Nursing Bottle

Lightweight 2-piece. Simply hold to breast – gradually extract milk into hygienic container which becomes nursing bottle. Dishwasher safe. Holds 3 ounces. Complete with nipple, seal, cover. A must for working mothers.

$18.00

Free & Dry™ Breast Care Shields

Helps prepare nipples for baby. Never a worry about leaking. Hides away inside your bra comfortably. Collects moisture – can't stain clothing. Pair in carry case.

$5.95

— — — — — — — — — **MONEY-BACK GUARANTEE** — — — — — — — —

Family-Time
Box 15129, Las Vegas, Nevada 89114

Please rush me the order below

Quantity	Product Name	Price	Total

Service & handling
$1.00 per order
(unless separately indicated)
Canada and out-of-country
add $1.25 for each item

Handling charge _____
Tax – if Nevada or Illinois _____
TOTAL _____

☐ Baby is expected _____ (months)
☐ Baby is here Age _____ ☐ 1st ☐ 2nd ☐ 3rd
Please charge to my Credit Card
Account No. _____
Mastercharge Interbank No. _____
Exp. Date Mo. _____ Year ____
☐ BankAmericard ☐ Mastercharge

Signature _____

Name _____

Address _____

City _____

State _____ Zip _____

Phone Number (area code) _____